FUSS AND FURY

OF NEO FEUDALISM

HARSH WILSON

Contents

Foreword

"Fuss and Fury of Neo-Feudalism" – The title itself is distinct and highly relevant in the neo-colonial era. As the work of an individual who contended for the prestigious Indian civil services, it is evident that it covers a 360-degree, multi-dimensional view of life in the 21st century. Harsh's departure from the status quo was not only revolutionary but also a painful process of transition from what he did not want, to what he wished for, and from what he wished for, to what he was not aware of; a journey from the unknown to the known and further to nowhere.

The book has an interactive narration and suits the requirements of a movie script. I hope this book can be produced into a movie someday. However, this is not just a book; it is an emotional journey of a human being in search of the real meaning of life. In every word and sentence of this book, I can see the impressions of knowledge Harsh has earned. This work breaks the traditional rules of writing, making the presentation soothing to read. Harsh's ideas present a contemporary view of the corporate world. He describes how corporate feudal lords can exploit personnel in the name of targets and goals for self-gain. Harsh appears to me as a modern Marxist who exposes and explodes the corporate rituals of programming human machines in the name of workaholism. He depicts how reforms are opposed by the very people they are meant to benefit. This book insists that unless reforms are revolutionized, they are not enforced. Many of the concepts used in this book by Harsh are handpicked from public administration, including the ivory tower, the spoils system, con artists, etc. He also introduces certain new ideas like the bro-code. His view on corporate corruption is an eye-opener to reality. His other views are also brutally realistic, including those on corporate romance and societal judgments.

As I went through the pages of this book, I was totally immersed in it. I can see the agony Harsh underwent and feel inspired by how he rose out of each of his issues. The surreal societal views on success have been challenged: do what you want to do, be free. For a learner like Harsh, every failure is a lesson and every lesson learned is a victory.

I am proud to be his teacher."

-**Krishna Pradeep**, Professor and Director, KP Group of Educational Institutions

Preface

Within these pages lies a narrative born of my journey within the corporate landscape of India. Rather than painting with broad strokes, I have chosen to illuminate my personal experiences, recognizing that while the essence of corporate culture may resonate universally, everyone's encounter is nuanced and unique. This endeavor not only speaks to those entrenched in corporate realms but also finds resonance with aspirants of Indian civil services navigating the intricacies of contemporary life.

Through my words, many will find reflections of their own daily struggles and triumphs. In an effort to honor the privacy and dignity of my former colleagues and the organizations they represent, the names and locations have been altered throughout this work. Rest assured; the integrity of the narrative remains steadfast.

The term *neo-feudalism* I used in my work does not arise from or relate to the definitions laid down by any other authors in either their academic orientations or non-academic references. This work is solely based on my own observations and experiences. This work also contains several references to my past, including my love life, the journey through civil services preparation, and the experiences of childhood, adolescence, and adult abuse and trauma. These topics, each, separately will be explored in more detail in my subsequent publications.

Harsh Wilson

Acknowledgments

Thank you from the deepest corners of my heart to everyone who helped turn my hobby of writing into authorship.

I would like to extend my heartfelt gratitude to my professor, Mr. Krishna Pradeep (KP), who has been instrumental in shaping the person I am today. He is a constant source of inspiration, with a depth of knowledge and a perspective on life that surpasses ordinary imagination. He has shown each of his students how to face failures with courage and rise above them. Just as Napoleon might not have existed without Rousseau, I would not be who I am without KP.

Special thanks to Ms. Sheri Velarde, who has encouraged me since we met in the US in 2023. Whenever I felt low in confidence due to fear of societal judgment, Ms. Velarde assured me that my work was worthy of being shared. She is an extraordinary person, and I feel incredibly fortunate to have met her. As an author of eighteen literary works so far, each a testament to her intellect and creativity, her validation gave me the courage to take the bold step towards my first publication. I wish her good health and cheer so she can continue to write, sketch, and showcase her many talents.

To my brother, Mr. Vishnu Vardhan, who tirelessly read through the lines of this book and encouraged me to persevere. He witnessed my struggle with PTSD following the tragedies described in this book and instilled in me the valor to expose the wrongdoings to the world. He insisted that the righteous must always speak up and stand for their rights.

To all those who reviewed my work multiple times and encouraged me to share this experience with the world, I am deeply grateful.

I. A Departure from Status Quo

In November 2018, in New Delhi, India, at the age of 28, I found myself at a crossroads during the intense rush of the country's most sought-after Indian civil services examination, which is often seen as a colonial legacy. I had already spent five solid years preparing for this prestigious exam by then. For many aspirants like me, it becomes an addiction and an obsession, persisting until either success is achieved or attempts are exhausted by age or number.

Such competitive examinations consume immense amounts of time and energy, often without us realizing it. We invest the most productive years of our youth analyzing government policies and crafting innovative solutions to contemporary crises. Coming from a well-to-do family, earning a living was not a necessity for me when I started my preparation; so, I relied mostly on freelance work to cover my minimal expenses.

I have always believed that for common public to live happier lives, those in powerful roles—whether sovereign or non-sovereign—must safeguard their interests through effective administration, policing, justice, healthcare, education, defense, and activism. I found my purpose within this community of responsible protectors in public life. Achieving this required a great deal of courage and sacrifice, and I have already dedicated many years to this pursuit. It was difficult to imagine putting a halt or a full stop to my ambitions.

However, there came a time when I had to confront the harsh reality that I was ensnared in an endless cycle of examination attempts, all while grappling with weighty issues at home. Decades of ongoing crises had pushed my family to the brink of financial ruin, demanding my focused intervention to rectify our circumstances. Each failure in the examination further chipped away at my self-confidence, instilling in me a growing anxiety. The mere thought of such an outcome filled me with profound regret.

Adding to that turmoil, a few months ago, I was abruptly abandoned by someone I deeply loved. A fully functional relationship ended without any explanation. This heartbreak shattered my faith in humanity and made me question my worth and path. I was engulfed in ethical dilemmas, stemming not only from career struggles and the recent breakup but also from my upbringing and the challenges I faced as a result.

To provide context, I come from a dysfunctional family where parenting was abusive, subjecting me to cruelty, incarceration, and discrimination from infancy. Each morning, I went to school with either a sore muscle, swollen lips, a skin rash, or a painful joint, and every night, I slept with the same ailments after enduring further abuse. I wish someone like Hagrid had come to save me. There was not a single day I can recall without physical punishment until I was fifteen, when I finally retaliated in self-defense. This led to a vindictive displacement of my goals within my already neglected career. The emotional abuse intensified, compounded by financial abuse during a crucial time when every child depends on parents at such age. I dealt with autism and hysteria during my childhood that heightened during adolescence. It took a great deal of effort to overcome these challenges and learn to cope with daily life by the time I reached my twenties.

In a society as traditional as India, a child often receives the same treatment from the community as they do from their parents. Thus, I grew up bullied, both at school and in my residential locality, adding to the abuse at home. The inaction of those who are supposed to protect children emboldens the unruly and ruthless elements of society to exploit and prey upon the vulnerable. These experiences impacted my social abilities, making me feel feral in human society, mistrustful of the world, and intolerant of injustice anywhere around.

The responsibilities I took on from a young age included raising my emotionally immature parents, handling my sibling, figuring out everything by myself, resolving household problems as the eldest child, helplessly watching as we lost ancestral property to relatives, and managing every consequence of my father's vices.

All these responsibilities above my age and capacity consumed me, causing me to neglect myself.

As a result, my great ambitions faced a complete collapse. My first career phase was derailed when I had to leave the aviation industry in my late adolescence, and now, in my late twenties, my second career phase in civil services faced a similar fate due to the lack of support and value for education in my family. When my initial goal was displaced, my distress migration in education led me to aimlessly pursue Bachelors in Business studies and began working as a Human Resources professional. I continued freelancing in HR, very occasionally during my civil services preparation while I also completed Masters in Public Administration with the spirit of public service. Additionally, I worked as a faculty member for over a year, teaching Public Administration and the Constitution, besides, providing content writing for general studies in civil services. I gained immense confidence and developed my personality through my civil services preparation, which shaped me into someone who stands up for others, even when standing alone. With that goal, which was the second one now displaced, I was shattered into pieces. I had no choice but to restart my HR career, competing with younger, fresher candidates in the market, which seemed daunting. On one hand, I felt I was on the verge of clearing the civil service exam and it seemed foolish to quit at this critical juncture. On the other hand, my patience was wearing thin, and practicality demanded attention. Harshly, I chose to cancel all my enrollments in various test series and sold most of my books and answer scripts, keeping only a few as souvenirs of my preparation. Knowledge remains a tacit asset that cannot be stolen.

Determined to excel in any field I chose, I left it to time to reveal whether this was a temporary or permanent change. For an ambitious person like me, there is likely no terminal goal. After years of unwavering focus on a single objective, I no longer feared failure. I held my head high, knowing my story was one of a path "less traveled." I took the flight back home, from Delhi to Bangalore, not yet sure how to reintegrate into the 'regular life' dictated by societal norms. Starting from scratch is always painful. I also had plans of leaving the country.

I consulted my well-wisher and the Director, KP sir, at the institute where I was coached for civil services. I am quite close to him informally. After narrowly missing qualifying each year, I asked him if I could work and study simultaneously. Each time, he denied, authoritatively asserting that I should stick to the exam and not dilute my preparation. Not just him, but several others had immense faith in my efforts. However, that year, I informed him of my decision: it was time to quit the preparation and address my long-pending personal issues.

KP: "Why not continue teaching and writing articles? That will keep you engaged with your studies and also provide financial support."

Me: "I do not want to be involved in anything related to studies right now, sir. It has become too depressing due to my current concentration issues."

KP: "You would not survive in the corporate world. You will get bored of it very soon."

Me: "I know, sir. I am trained to serve in a public capacity, but I do not know how I will manage in the corporate. I want to gain some experience and then move out of the country."

KP: "Nice! Are you planning to go back to Malaysia?"

Me: "No, sir. I may settle down in the West."

KP: "Good luck! Would you aim at the civil services in the West?"

Me: "I do not know anything as of now sir. I do not want to plan anything for my life. I think I am done with it, sir. Please wish me well."

My well-wishers and close ones knew that I would struggle to fit under any authority, given my activist stance and agitated mind. Despite this, I decided to go against the grain. I did not know what lay ahead, but I was ready to embrace whatever challenges came my way. My thoughts remained idealistic, and my ambitions were still high. Yet, as I prepared to enter the job market, my assets were:

1. **Academics**: An excellent profile, with a BA (Hons) in International Business Management from abroad, complemented by global projects and an international internship in Human Resource Management, and an MA in Public Administration from Delhi.

2. **Employment**: Experience in teaching and content writing across diverse subjects such as Public Administration and General Studies, along with some freelance HR experience.

3. **Miscellaneous**: Visible political associations and social activism, as well as hobbies like writing and singing.

I meticulously included all these details on my resume, knowing I had honest answers to any potential questions. I chose to approach a company I was familiar with, having accompanied a friend to his interview there in 2013, though he unfortunately was not selected. The company, a Californian firm referred hereafter to as CF, specialized in digital engineering services and software products, situated in Bellandur. With prestigious clients like Apple and Google, CF stood out in the industry. I applied for the position of Recruiter-Human Resources within their Talent Acquisition Group, known as TAG.

Internally, I was far from okay. I silenced my heart in that moment, rationalizing my decisions to cope with the challenges at home. Stepping into CF was not about fulfilling my dreams, but rather navigating the circumstances I found myself in. I refused to subscribe to the defeatist notion that life is inherently unfair and crushes aspirations. While life may throw unfairness our way, our response to it defines our character. I firmly believed in the power of time; it has the capacity to both build and destroy. However, whether that construction or destruction occurs depends entirely on our attitude.

This world presents us with numerous challenges, often thrust upon us without mental preparation. Embracing these challenges is what distinguishes a common man from a leader. I embraced it. It was another chapter in my life, another experience to add to my journey. By stepping away from the sanctity of my past and embracing the life of an ordinary person among ordinary people, I disrupted the status quo and embarked on a new phase of personal growth.

II. Collective-Sycophancy Welcomes

On the day of my first visit, when I walked-in on November 21st, the recruitment team was away at a client meeting, so I could not meet anyone. However, I encountered **Romeo**, a manager from a specific project, during his snack break downstairs. He informed me of the team's whereabouts and suggested I return the following day. On November 22nd, 2018, I met with **Gary**, the Manager of the TAG Team, at CF. After informing the team of my arrival, I was directed to wait on the third floor.

Romeo noticed me waiting and greeted me with a smile, commenting, "So, you are finally here! Been waiting long?"

Me: "No, that's okay."

After Romeo left, **Indira**, a senior executive, called me into Gary's cabin. She formally introduced me to Gary and then left the room.

Me: "Good afternoon! I apologize for only bringing my resume; I couldn't carry my entire file."

Gary: "That is alright, please have a seat." (Smiles)

Gary: "How did you hear about the vacancies?"

Me: "If there are vacancies in the recruitment team, you should let me know. I came directly to inquire."

Gary: "Ah, that's good. Yes, we do have vacancies. We are looking for recruiters."

Me: "That is great!"

Gary: "How are you familiar with our firm?"

Me: "I accompanied a friend to an interview here in 2013. Since then, I have been aware of the company."

Gary: "Nice, Harsh! Have you worked in recruitment before?"

Me: "Yes, I have international internship and some freelance experience in recruitment."

Gary: "That's wonderful! Could you please wait outside for a moment?"

Me: "Of course, Gary."

After a brief wait, I was called back into the cabin. Indira was seated, and Gary was on a bean bag. I took a seat before both.

Gary: "You have an impressive profile. Could you share something interesting about yourself?"

I elaborated on everything mentioned in my resume, including my hobbies and life outside of work/studies. The conversation flowed smoothly.

Indira: "He was an active member in politics, Gary." (Checking the resume in a frantic manner) "He could be a threat to the company, for sure."

Me: "If a corporate businessman can become a President of a powerful country, how could my political associations be a threat to the company?"

Indira: "Look! You have a 'fluctuating' career."

Me: (Politely) "It is not fluctuating; you can call it 'diverse.'"

Indira: "Whatever! Your profile reflects that you are creative. You may easily get bored with this job and cause problems."

Me: (Softly) "I came with a long-term commitment. Sticking to one goal, as you can see from my resume, despite repetitive failures, demonstrates my determination. It is not a joke."

Indira looked at Gary in embarrassment, and I turned to him.

Gary: "You seem very convincing. You have great communication skills and creativity."

Me: "Thank you!"

Gary: "There is a lot of public administration content on your profile."

Me: "Yes."

Gary: "Are you okay with joining as a fresher?"

Me: "Thank you! But may I ask why?"

Gary: "Your teaching and freelance experience may not be relevant here. The only thing we can consider is your Management Graduation and international HR internship."

Indira: "And that too not in India. We cannot perform background verification."

Me: "You always can."

Indira: "Yeah, but…"

Gary: (To Indira) "Wait!" (To me) "The pay would also be low for a fresher."

Me: "May I please know the pay?"

Gary: "About x.x LPA. Are you fine with that?"

Me: "We can negotiate."

Indira: "You may have to work on Saturdays at times. Are you ready for that?"

Me: "If needed at times, I'll extend my hand to the team and be here."

Gary: "It does not generally happen, but yes, all of us may have to come in depending on the requirements. You'll receive incentives, though."

Me: "Not an issue!"

Gary: "You'll receive a call soon. I want to introduce you to the Assistant Vice President (AVP). You can discuss the rest with him. He will give the confirmation."

Spot approval from Gary made me happy. He pushed my profile to AVP named **Krishna** (who introduced himself as **Kris**) for confirmation. Interestingly, the formal conversation turned into a discussion with Indira right in the interview room. I sensed immediately after the discussion that while I may have been unaware of it, a clash between me and Indira was inevitable in the coming days.

I received a call from Indira that same evening before her log-out time. She asked me to come to the office on the 26th at 3 PM to meet Mr. Kris. I reported on time, and Gary instructed me to speak plainly (keeping in mind my interaction with Indira).

Gary: "See, Harsh! You quite impressed me. We need you and your skills on the team. I am vouching for you! Please come with me, let me show you Kris's cabin."

Me: "Sure! I appreciate that. I won't let you down."

I followed Gary, who introduced me to Kris.

Me (smiling and polite): "Good afternoon! How are you, Kris?"

Kris (clearing his throat): "I'm good! How about you? Please take a seat."

Me: "Thank you! I'm good, Kris."

Kris: "So, tell me, why recruitment?"

Me: "Recruitment found me. It is a perfect fit according to my SWOT analysis. I successfully closed requirements for the most complicated clients of my past companies."

Kris: "Hmmm! That is impressive. How did you get here? Do you have a vehicle?"

Me: "No, I use public transport for now. I was in Delhi until recently and do not have my own vehicle yet." (I had a vehicle but I said this to potentially receive transportation allowance).

Kris: "Great! I started my career similarly. I see myself in you. Is your place about 30-40 minutes to Bellandur? You stay in Koramangala, right?"

Me: "H.S.R Layout. It takes nearly 35 minutes by a two-wheeler. I usually book Rapido or Drivezy."

Kris: "Good! What do your parents do?"

Me: "Dad works in print media, and my mom is a music teacher and dubbing artist in the Sandalwood industry."

Kris: "You come from a wonderful family. I like your nature— soft, polite, and always smiling. Gary, too, is like that and has been with us for over 10 years. I think you will work well under his supervision."

Me: "Nice to know!"

Kris: "So, what are you expecting in terms of salary?"

Me: "Anything reasonable that wouldn't push me into the culture of poverty."

Kris: "But give me a figure." (He did not catch the humor in "culture of poverty.")

Me: "At least x.x LPA since I am not entirely new to recruitment."

Kris: "How long can you work with us?"

Me: "I am here with a long-term commitment."

Kris: "How long is that? And what if you decide to go back to civil services attempts?"

Me: "Your concern is valid, Kris. I can give a verbal commitment of two years. Regarding civil services, I might have to let it go due to personal compulsions. If not public service, there is no point in staying in India, as that was my primary reason for returning from Malaysia."

Kris: "So, you have plans to go back to Malaysia?"

Me: "No, I might move to the West with sufficient corporate experience. Maybe two years here will suffice."

Kris: "Will you settle in the corporate sector?"

Me: "I don't think so. After a few years of corporate experience, the West offers lateral entry into their civil services, and I plan to pursue that."

Kris: "That is good. You have a vision in everything you do. We can offer you either an HR Consultant role or a Senior Member role. I will discuss with Gary what he needs for his team."

Me: "Thank you. Sure!"

Kris: "Nice talking to you, Harsh. Wishing you all the best! Gary will contact you."

Me: "Thank you very much! It was nice meeting you!"

I went home and received a call from Gary the next afternoon, on November 27th. He congratulated me on my selection, and we discussed the offer details. The negotiation was interesting:

1. The offer was on a contractual basis until March 31st, likely influenced by Indira's intervention due to her wariness of my confident and straightforward attitude.
2. The role was HR Senior Member of the Talent Acquisition Group.
3. The initial package was set at x.x LPA, with a promised revision in four months as the financial year to end on March 31st.

I liked the company and its projects. Working with such prestigious clients would enhance my resume. I convinced myself not to miss this growth opportunity, despite knowing that the HR department, being predominantly female in general, might pay less to a male employee. I accepted the offer anyway. I was aware that contractual employees were often denied incentives, salary hikes, leaves, and other benefits that regular employees enjoyed, allowing companies to hire and fire at will.

Indira congratulated me over the phone that evening and asked me to collect the offer letter on November 28th and start the same day. I received my offer letter via email and noticed an error in the joining date, which Gary promptly corrected. He advised me to relax until my official login credentials were generated. Indira, acting sweetly, told me the job was manageable, with work coming in bursts rather than continuously. Unaware that the office provided food, I brought my lunch from home, which surprised the team. Later, I received an email instructing me to complete my joining formalities the next morning, November 29th.

Intellectual "Western" Rights

As I completed my joining formalities, I could not help but smile at the tactically crafted terms and conditions. The Californian firm claimed ownership of any invention or discovery made by employees during their employment, whether inside or outside the office. This reminded me of how Western companies exploit third-world countries through intellectual property rights (IPR) laws. The documents clearly stated that any invention or discovery would be the company's property as long as the employee was associated with it. Reflecting on the economic colonialism akin to the *Dunkel Draft*,[1] I realized the extent of this exploitation. When I mentioned to others that I read the document carefully, I was told that most people did not ever bother. Nevertheless, I finished quickly and accepted the harsh reality of this exploitation.

---

[1] Biswajit Dhar, C Niranjan Rao, 'Dunkel Draft on TRIPS: Complete Denial of Developing Countries' Interests' [1992] 27(6) Economic and Political Weekly 275-278.

III. Devoted Workaholism

On Saturday, December 1, 2018, a mega recruitment drive for freshers was organized at the Bellandur branch. The day before, on November 30, Indira briefed me on the skills required from the candidates, though she did not provide details about the associated projects. I took notes on her instructions and prepared for the recruitment cycle.

I arrived at the office at 9 AM. Candidates were already waiting, and their numbers were increasing rapidly. The seating capacity was limited, forcing me to start conducting interviews without first observing how the manager and senior executive would handle such a large event. I was unfamiliar with the projects and processes. Gary arrived at 9:30 AM and quickly began supervising me, showing me how to select candidates for each project as per their requirements. The crowd swelled to 480, and we had to accelerate the process.

Gary and I were the only ones managing this massive turnout. Indira called to check on the progress and informed me she would arrive within an hour. She joined us by 11 AM, by which time we had processed about 170 candidates already. Gary struggled to guide me while speeding up the process, but we pushed through. Lunchtime passed, and we still had hundreds of candidates to interview. Gary asked about lunch, but I suggested we focus on finishing the work and eat later, as it felt inhumane to eat while the candidates, who had traveled far, were starving. Our office was in a posh locality, and nearby affordable outlets for the candidates were closed. Gary appreciated my consideration. Indira handled only two batches of 60 candidates each, revealing her tendency to avoid the bulk of the work.

We wrapped up the process by 3:40 PM. After sorting and processing the day's data, we finally ordered food and ate lunch in the cafeteria at 4:15 PM. I was happy with how the day had gone but the important take-aways were that the team and its operations were highly disorganized; only the ones who felt responsible were overburdened but the others who were making time & money on the job, for instance, Indira, took great pleasure in shifting responsibility onto others.

During my previous HR experience and internships, I worked on IT recruitment for highly experienced candidates, typically hiring only 3-4 candidates each month. That routine talent hunt was very different from my role at CF. Here, I handled a diverse range of recruitments, including technical, non-technical, medical, IT, and mapping roles. I was thrilled to be contributing to the employment of many young people, creating livelihoods for hundreds each day.

The TAG team had four members before I joined. Gary led the team and managed project requirements. **Aparna**, another team member, focused solely on experienced IT profiles at the Bellandur CF. The fourth member was the Deputy Manager of TAG. The following week, Gary informed me of a new assignment.

"Harsh," Gary said, "you may need to assist our Deputy Manager, Mr. **Sagar**, at the Marathahalli branch. You will only need to be at the Bellandur office during walk-ins and other major events."

"Alright, Gary. Where is it?" I asked.

"It is nearby, in Marathahalli. I will take you there soon," he replied.

Indira had mentioned that I would enjoy working with Sagar, and I hoped she was right, as I wanted my work to be enjoyable. That same afternoon, I was taken to Marathahalli. There were 17 fresher positions to be filled for Google that week, and some candidates from Saturday's interviews needed to be processed for the client round. The final interviews were scheduled for Tuesday, with on-site personnel invited. I coordinated between the on-site team and TAG, ensuring all candidates were invited for the final round. Sagar left at 6 PM, but I stayed until 8:30 PM to ensure all interviews were completed. I was praised for providing more candidates than required by the client, which boosted my confidence and set a positive tone for my future at the company.

I was the lynchpin for the TAG team, bridging the Bellandur and Marathahalli offices. My responsibilities included managing both fresher and experienced candidate requirements up to the selection process. Initially, I was not involved in salary negotiations or issuing offer letters. This division of labor was an understanding between Sagar and me, ensuring our workdays ran smoothly. We spent countless hours innovating to improve organization, as the team had previously struggled with efficiency due to its small size.

Sagar, who had a network of colleagues including managers and admin staff from various projects, took on the role of my mentor. The Marathahalli office was intense; once inside, you were so immersed in work that the outside world ceased to exist. With projects tied to production, time management and punctuality for their employees in respective projects were crucial. Sagar guided me through each project meticulously within a week. His informal relationships with everyone helped me understand the projects quickly, despite the lack of formal introductions to each compartment.

We often worked Saturdays and occasionally Sundays to meet our closure targets. My dedication shifted entirely to my work, making the office feel like my primary home. Sagar and I regularly spent over 12 hours a day at work. I discovered my workaholic side, thanks to Sagar's mentorship. As John Crossby said, "Mentoring is a brain to pick, an ear to listen, and a push in the right direction." Sagar embodied this philosophy.

Sagar, ten years my senior, always introduced me as his colleague rather than his subordinate. Despite facing frequent insults and office politics, he remained dedicated to his work. He kept a resignation letter drafted in his email but never wavered in his commitment. Sagar's resilience was admirable. Coming from a poor financial and social background, Sagar never imagined he would ever speak English or work in an MNC. He earned his MBA in HR through sheer hard work, and he respected every achievement.

Sagar's humility extended to everyone, including the office's housekeeping staff, with whom he often shared conversations and meals. I once wrote a poem about him that resonated throughout CF, earning him well-deserved praise, and reflecting my admiration for him.

He is a fusion of level-5 transformational leadership and
Theory-Z transactionalleadership[2]

He is a mercury gel that can flow
smooth among any-'body'

He is a logical being who can
turn anything hard into easy

---

[2] Citlalli Rocio Flores-Rodriguez, Jose Sanchez-Gutierrez and Jorge Pelayo-Maciel, 'Leadership and Management Theories and Bridging the Gap between these Theories--A Literature Review' (2018) 16(2) American Society for Competitiveness.

His humor has bold heights of hilarious self-humiliation regardless of his stature

His generosity to give out whole of his knowledge to the seeking is extraordinary

His gracious interaction in coming down from his managerial position to the level of any menial worker is astonishing

Hence the deserving title- "The Management Guru", **the Peter Drucker[3] of CF**

We were completely consumed by our work. Sagar, with his unhappy personal life, spent most of his time at the office, preferring it over going home. Before I joined the firm, he frequented clubs and lounges after the work. I, too, had no reason to rush home. My evenings were filled with sadness, as I roamed like a zombie, weeping over a heartbreak and the betrayal of someone I thought was my soulmate. Without exams to prepare for, I usually stayed at the office until 8:30 PM, averagely and arrived around 8 AM. Despite coming in late, Sagar always stayed until after I left, once we started working together.

We achieved a lot with minimal resources. Sagar moved from his cabin to sit in my bay, which was spacious and lively, becoming

---

[3] Timothty S Kiessling, Glenn R Richey, 'Examining the theoretical inspirations of a management guru: Peter F. Drucker and the Austrian School of Economics,' (2004) 42(10) Management Decision 1269-1283.

a social hub for colleagues from various projects. I entertained everyone by mimicking people, from the AVP to housekeeping staff. Even at home, I remained available for work. Gary often assigned tasks post-9 PM, such as scheduling interviews, always with my consent though. Sagar and I often worked from home after 11:30 PM, and he would find me replying to office emails at 3 AM. My dedication, previously directed at preparing for civil service exams, was now channeled into my work.

When other commitments such as dealing with quarrels & hardships at home kept me from the office, I conducted video interviews. At one instance, Kris and **Manish**, the Delivery Team Manager, asked me to work on 12 high-profile requirements at 9:30 PM, needing interviews scheduled for the immediate next day. It was a strategic business move to acquire the workforce of a competitor whose project had ramped down. I stayed until 11 PM to complete the task successfully. I also vividly remember the immediate requirement on December 24th for several Team Leaders/Pod Leads, with a deadline of January 2nd. That week was hectic, working full days through Christmas and New Year, but we met the target by January 7th.

Sagar and I often played music and sang along to make work enjoyable. After Saturday drive-ins, we watched movies in the conference room with the projector on, during late lunches. Together, we transformed the organization. I suggested various improvements to our work culture, which Sagar embraced being in the capacity of a Deputy Manager. One significant change was to digitize the candidate database, replacing the security register at the entrance. This made tracking candidate details and selection/rejection processes much more efficient. We set up systems to immediately detect any data manipulation within the team.

I created innovative videos about the company to make walk-in drives more appealing and helped candidates feel confident during interviews. I spent many nights making presentations and videos to boost the recruitment team's morale. I motivated underpaid team members, especially Aparna and Sagar, to advocate for their incentives, highlighting that the recruitment team is a revenue-generating entity. My ideas were well-received, and within the team, we had the freedom to execute them.

Sagar often told me that I modernized the team, transforming an ill-equipped group into a progressive unit. It was a new world and experience for me, with my dedication to books turning into a dedication to work. I was happy to see my education bringing about progressive reforms. While I once aimed to execute my ideas in civil service, either in a ministry, department, or district, I now saw a company benefiting from them.

IV. Peaceful Vs Harmless

Reforms do not last without recognition and appreciation. They also falter in the presence of cowards. Throughout history, there is a key observation to be made about exploitation: if one is harmless, exploitation persists as long as the person is alive. There is a significant difference between being harmless and being peaceful.

"You cannot call yourself peaceful unless you're capable of retaliating against any violence. If you are not capable of such retaliation, you are harmless."

— Unknown

This phrase holds profound truth. To those stuck in their comfort zones and cowardly lifestyles, I sound disingenuous. Nevertheless, the statement carries a powerful meaning. Every major revolution and war in human history occurred to bring peace and attain freedom. One must be ready to wage war to achieve peace. War need not always be violent. This philosophy often eludes the common mind, necessitating a leader to mobilize the masses. Now, let us identify who was harmless in this firm and who strived to attain peace.

Gary is a down-to-earth person in his personal life, leading a simplistic lifestyle. He is a lawyer by education, an environmentalist by passion, and a communist by ideology. An armchair intellectual, he lives alone in a large flat and remains unmarried in his forties, having reached a state of self-actualization. Gary is a hardworking individual capable of handling immense workloads single-handedly. He has been an inspiration to Sagar for his patience in the face of exploitation, office politics, and oppression. While I admired his patience and intellect to some extent, I never liked his attitude of accepting oppression with a smile. He remained silent even when his potential was exploited or his team's self-respect was hurt. Patience to this level was ludicrous.

Indira exploited Gary significantly. She reported late to the office each day and, despite being a graduate from a Tier-I college in the city, she was inefficient in her work. Initially part of the core HR team, she was expelled due to laxity and multiple errors. Gary offered her asylum in his cabin, attempting to teach her recruitment tasks. Despite her potential to judge people well and work efficiently, she consistently complained and failed to focus on her tasks. This left the burden of work on Gary and Sagar.

Aparna was a calm employee who completed her work and left quietly, maintaining good relations with Kris and enjoying a smooth work life. Her area of recruitment which was to deal with the experienced core-IT professionals, was isolated from the rest of the team.

Sagar, on the other hand, was a desperate employee who badly needed his job. He faced numerous hardships to get there, having previously worked for a consultancy that paid him negligibly. To his dismay, he was underpaid even at CF, following the precedent set by his previous employment. Despite his job insecurity, he always kept a draft of his resignation letter ready, unable to bear the conditions at work. Hailing from North Karnataka and belonging to a backward caste, he faced social discrimination even in the modern corporate structure. Due to his financial situation, he could not raise his voice against any injustices. I and Sagar happened to be at loggerheads most of the times in this very aspect. I pushed him always to stand up for himself but he was never courageous enough.

Overall, while some in the firm tried to maintain peace and drive progress, others exploited these efforts, highlighting the stark contrasts in the workplace.

Dirty Picture

Every day brought a new shock as I witnessed the ill-treatment of the recruitment team. Due to our manager's lack of confidence, every other team played games with the TAG team. In terms of respect, we were only slightly above the security department. **Raghu**, a project manager heading two US projects and a close associate of Mr. Kris, had a long history of moral policing and vigilantism against TAG. Sagar informed me about him during my first week.

The week before I joined, Raghu escalated an issue to Kris, accusing the recruitment team of irresponsibly leaving resumes scattered and lights on at the end of the day, disrupting second-shift employees. TAG was warned of severe action without a chance to defend ourselves, essentially reducing us to housekeeping duties.

Romeo, the first person I met before even I joined, was another thorn in our side. As an off-site manager for an Apple client project, he escalated an issue during my first week, accusing TAG of inhumanely making candidates wait too long. This created a cold war atmosphere. Gary and Sagar demanded evidence, and Romeo cited my own interview. Gary called me to ask if I had waited long, but I had been given preference and hardly waited at all. After this, Sagar warned me to be cautious, as our team's leadership was too weak to defend us effectively.

Therefore, these two managers, Raghu and Romeo treated TAG personnel like a soccer ball, tossing responsibilities and blame our way.

Mr. Kris's visits to the Marathahalli branch were like Polo tours, involving long, unproductive meetings with close associates that disrupted our work. On one busy day, Raghu was engaged in one of these pointless chats with Kris. They claimed to discuss projects, but it was mostly gossip (proved in below conversation). That day, Sagar was summoned and interrogated unfairly by Raghu, even though Kris was the actual reporting authority.

Conversation:

Raghu: "Your team is the most unorganized one. We are ashamed of your work. You do not maintain data sheets and have never met your targets."

Sagar: "Kris, who is this person to question me?"

Kris: "I have the same questions as he does. Please answer."

Sagar: "I know my work and what my team is doing. I would not discuss this in front of an outsider, who is not related to recruitment."

Raghu: "Mind your behavior. You are nothing here; better keep that in mind."

Sagar: "Kris, you can check the data sheets on my desktop. Since Harsh joined, we have digitized everything."

Kris: "You still have not explained why closures aren't on time."

Sagar: "We are understaffed, lack devices, have no space for interviews, having to work on weekends to meet targets and our pay packages are not competitive in the market. There are many issues, but we have never had a chance to discuss them."

Kris: "Okay, you may leave, Sagar!"

Sagar emerged distressed out of that room and took me to the cafeteria to explain what had happened. He was furious about the interference from outsiders in our team matters. I was equally upset, knowing Raghu, who had zero knowledge about management and recruitment, was lecturing us. We felt ridiculed.

A few days later, the delivery team, led by Manish, summoned Sagar to explain why he could not deliver results. They were pressured by the Google client, who noted that CF was not providing human resources compared to competitors. Sagar confronted the interference in our team's daily operations, but he was warned of consequences and sent out. Gary was warned to keep his team in check but never took a stand for us, instead suppressing us further. The higher-ups even threatened to dissolve the recruitment team and outsource its functions. Every kind of toxic management could be seen from the above. Micromanagement, poor resource allocation, playing favorites, withholding information, being unavailable to discuss issues, involving outsiders, and dividing people to keep the position of authority.[4] Leadership is often misconceived by the mediocre minds as position of authority whereas in reality, it is a responsibility.

Another incident I learned about was that Sagar had been given a cabin next to the security gate before I joined, due to his poor relationship with management. This symbolized the extent of the mistreatment and lack of respect our team endured.

Further Atrocities

When I joined the team, the conditions were deplorable. Basic facilities like laptops and mobile phones, essential for achieving targets, were not provided. The landline connections in our bays were constantly faulty, disconnecting abruptly each day and never functioning properly until the next day, only to repeat the same issues. When I informed Sagar about this, he showed me his personal phone, which he had arranged for official purposes years ago. Following his example, I converted one of my personal numbers into an official one, paying the bills myself. Gary

---

4 Bill Feruzan, Lori Tribble, and others, 'Just Let Me Do My Job!: Exploring the Impact of Micromanagement on IT Professionals' [2021] 52(3) Association for Computing Machinery <https://doi-org.liverpool.idm.oclc.org/10.1145/3481629.3481635> accessed on 5th May 2023.

promised reimbursement from the team's budget, but it never happened despite monthly expense reports sent via email.

Requests for devices like laptops and headphones, crucial for conducting candidate tests and video conferences, were consistently ignored. We had to borrow these devices from other projects, only to return them mid-task when the lenders needed them back, disrupting our work.

Sagar and I repeatedly asked Gary to demand these basic requirements from higher management. Gary, however, was too soft with the management, never raising demands despite his own suffering. He often yelled at us to shut us up, saying he had worked under the same conditions for over ten years without complaining and expected us to do the same to "survive." He would badmouth Kris, Manish, and other seniors behind their backs but never dared to confront them. This behavior frustrated Sagar, who, due to personal commitments, refrained from open confrontation. Instead, he would get drunk and vent to close friends. This coping mechanism worked for him, as he was not from a tech-savvy generation. TAG failed to understand that new generations in the workplace could not follow outdated, Luddite techniques.

A significant issue was the lack of Job Descriptions (JDs), an essential service for the hiring team. Requirements were communicated via email, specifying only the number of positions and target dates without details on skills or pay scales. Managers at the Google client location would provide these details over the phone if contacted. In my previous HR-Recruiter roles overseas as well as in India, communication was professional and harmonious, with clear and detailed JDs provided for every requirement. Gary never raised concerns about this, leading to irregular and unclear functioning. Projects directed us to schedule interviews regardless of salary expectations, leading to vacant positions and blaming the hiring team for not providing suitable candidates.

Another major issue was the lack of space for large recruitment drives. We had to wait for free office space on weekends, often working without pay, violating labor laws and Article 23 of the Indian Constitution, which prohibits forced labor. I informed Gary that our team was experiencing horrendous conditions. Despite his cursing of the delivery team, he could do nothing practical. I told him I could not work every weekend without pay, as it was financially unviable due to additional expenses like food and fuel not being reimbursed. Gary, being a lawyer, was powerless to argue effectively. Reluctantly, he arranged a meeting with the delivery team, including Sagar and me. The personnel at the Google location suggested holding interviews in the open parking area opposite the office, which was impractical due to security concerns and potential public nuisance. All three of us were enraged hearing that. The area was always heavily guarded by central armed police forces and state police security forces due to the proximity of a Union Minister's residence. I explained to the others on the video conference that holding interviews in that ground space would block public property, such as the road, as the number of interviewees would be in the hundreds. The constant shouting of names and paperwork loitering would create a public nuisance and eventually result in law-and-order issues. The people on the other side did not understand a word of what I was saying. They were annoyed and started to mock me. One of them, **Shiva**, sarcastically asked me what law and order meant, laughing as he spoke. I explained that the recruitment team could face criminal penalties for breaching the security protocol of a Union Minister. Gary understood my point and firmly denied holding interviews in that ground as a concluding statement. Then they asked us to come up with a solution for the space crunch issue. I proposed a leave rotation system, suggesting that all other off-site projects work on Saturdays and Sundays and take their week off on Mondays and Tuesdays, thereby providing us the space to hold drives on Mondays and Tuesdays. I was immediately told to shut up because I was proposing efficient managerial skills they were unfamiliar with. They had no solution or intention to accept remedies from our side and wanted us to continue suffering.

"Considering other man's viewpoint is decency."

-George Orwell

Fourthly, the pay scales offered to candidates were so low that CF's offers were looked down upon in the market. A French firm (referred to as FF hereafter) was offering lucrative jobs to candidates, closing more positions. The management asked us to obtain a pay-slip from the competitor's employees to prove this, despite already knowing the situation. We produced a pay-slip of a fresher pay-scale in the same month, but there was no response.

Fifthly, the TAG Team size at FF was eleven, whereas ours was only five. They had specialized each team member with a specific requirement allocation, whereas CF had a highly unorganized work culture.

Lastly, the common online sheets of requirements were updated without intimation via email, leading to increased vacancies. Each morning, the numbers changed, and we were left wondering and scrambling to meet the ends. Even if a requirement was ceased, it was not communicated to us professionally.

Cowardice: The Root Cause

I constantly asked Sagar why the team remained silent instead of raising issues with CF Indian headquarters in Noida about the appalling attitude of the Production and Delivery teams in Bangalore. He said they were waiting for the right time, which I doubted would ever come. Both the manager and deputy manager were cowards in varying degrees, confined to their comfort zones despite years of experience. They still carried job insecurities, and I pitied such cowardice. My team chose to be harmless and patient despite repeated attacks on their self-respect.

Bullies target defenseless and voiceless subjects to establish their dominance. A bully never stops until retaliated against. Their nature is to harm others to show power. Like in the political scenario in the country, the perpetrators in power start with unnecessary agendas such as Ghar-Wapsi, then escalate to demolishing religious sites and lynching innocent citizens. They sponsor assassinations of dissenters, turn universities into battlefields, and eventually implement draconian measures so as to evacuate with policies such as NRC. When protested, they respond with arrests under terroristic charges and violence. What will it take to end these atrocities? We must come out of cowardice and retaliate through all possible legal means. Be it in the company or the country, struggle is the only solution. Nobody can live peacefully until we fight to attain that peace. Being harmless is not an option, even in a democracy. Democracy is about rights and duties. Those in their comfort zones become the most affected victims as consequences pile up. By then, it is too late to retaliate.

V. Revolutionary Past

It was in October 2016 when I narrowly missed qualifying for the Mains in the Civil Services Examination by six marks. Seeking a change, I moved to Bhubaneswar for a short period of three months. During this time, I tried my hand at teaching, but it did not provide the break I needed as it still revolved around academics and studies. To divert my mind from the seriousness of life, I joined a Global Local Company (GLC) that serviced clients like Airtel and Amazon. I applied for an HR-Recruiter position, but since the vacancies were only opening in January 2017, I was offered a temporary role as a Customer Relationship Officer (CRO).

The interview process was rigorous, with seven to nine rounds designed to eliminate the intense competition. It included JAM (Just a Minute), essay writing, Pearson's Versant test, aptitude tests, telephonic interviews, situational rounds, and face-to-face interviews. I found the process enjoyable. Based on our performance, candidates were allocated to either Amazon or Airtel. Amazon required exceptional communication and convincing skills for their non-voice customer support, while Airtel handled voice processes and took in lower-scoring candidates. I was placed with Amazon. Despite not needing the job, I took it knowing I would soon quit to prepare for my next Civil Services attempt in 2017.

From day one, I formed a friendly rapport with the recruitment team, which was my tribe. Training commenced with cab facilities provided only during night and early morning shifts, but no food was served.

I take pride in becoming a "pain in the butt" for the management from the start. My education taught me to identify problems and provide solutions, which sometimes was mistaken for ego issues. However, it was not about ego; it was about standing up against wrongdoings and expecting accountability.

The first issue arose when our batch was not given offer letters despite the initiation of joining formalities. I demanded that we receive our offer letters before proceeding with any formalities. This led to a discussion with the HR teams, who requested a week to arrange the letters for the entire batch

Fredy: "Man! You went places at a young age, got empowered, and started questioning everything."

Me: "Thank you! It is not just about going places; it is about learning from them."

Fredy: "Why is the offer letter so important to you before signing the joining documents?"

Me: "Because it is lawful to have my offer letter first."

Fredy (laughs): "Lawful! Nice!"

With this, I became known across the entire office even before my first day of work. People began treating me with respect, though some in management sensed an undercurrent of resistance. However, the training period felt like a honeymoon phase. Our batch was a tight-knit group, filled with fun and camaraderie. We discussed politics, shared food, and interests, took pictures, danced, sang, went on outings, boozed, and more. It felt like being back in college, but this time with a paycheck.

In the very first week, batch members started missing their early morning cabs as their drivers could not find the addresses and left without picking up employees. The Team Leader, who was a local and indifferent to the non-locals staying in hostels, was supposed to address this issue. Instead, he warned latecomers of consequences but did not try to resolve the underlying problem. He yelled that the cab issue was not his concern and that he was only focused on maintaining discipline to ensure productivity. His authoritarian attitude prevented batchmates from freely conversing with him.

One day, I missed the cab as well and had to spend my own money on an auto-rickshaw. I arrived at the office in a disturbed mood. Surprisingly, the team leader did not dare confront me. After the shift, I took a stand for my colleagues. I asked the trainer, **Noela** about the Employee Relations HR to discuss the issue. I demanded monetary compensation of ten times what I had spent and insisted that this issue should not recur. I was naturally doing all this out of a legal sense. This automatically positioned me as a de facto leader, replacing the team leader's authority. People started approaching me with their issues, and I felt honored. Some batchmates even started calling me "mysterious."

A week later, the induction orientation began, led by Employee Relations HR, **Kavitha**, who was already impressed by my leadership in the cab issue. She briefed us on the number of working days and hours per week and the leave entitlements. I was the only one knowledgeable about basic labor laws. I smiled at her whenever I sensed exploitation. She asked to meet me at the end of the day. I pointed out that 48 hours per week is the legal limit for employment, and any work beyond that should be compensated with overtime pay. This company was engaging employees for 54 hours per week without extra pay. I explained that if a company wants its employees to work for six days a week, it should limit the hours to 8 per day, or if it wants them to work 9 hours a day, it should limit the workweek to 5 days to equate to the legal working hours in the legislation.

Kavitha: "I cannot do anything, Harsh. I am following the company's policies."

Me: "I know. As long as people are ignorant, this goes on. Do not worry, I am not going to educate people on this."

Kavitha: "You are really different. I have never seen such a person before."

Me: "I know. Thank you!"

There were no leaves during the 45-day training period as per the company policy. After the induction, some batchmates expressed concerns about needing leave for graduation exams. They convinced me to talk to Kavitha on their behalf. My batch trainer, Noela, was furious that I was bypassing her, but this responsibility should have fallen to the team leader. Given that batchmates were approaching me, I felt justified in my actions, though my formal relationship with Noela suffered as a result. She had the authority to decide if I continued or was thrown out of the company, but I did not care much since I planned to return to my studies soon.

One day, a batchmate was unwell and was not granted permission to go home. I planned to discuss this as well. **Faisal**, a colleague, and a good friend of mine joined me during my discussion with the HR to show solidarity with me. I put forward the issues seriously, and Kavitha approved half-day permissions for those with exams. The unwell batchmate was sent to the sick room. I was happy with these achievements and thanked profusely by my batchmates. With each achievement, I felt as happy as pre-independent India felt with the successes of Champaran Satyagraha, Kheda Satyagraha and Ahmedabad Mill Stike.

Kavitha: "Harsh! I did you a favor. What are you giving me in return?"

Me: "Please, go ahead. What can this small employee do for you, Ms. HR?"

Kavitha: "Mr. To-be-HR, you owe me an ice cream treat."

Faisal: "Wait! Is that a date?"

Kavitha: "Faisal, shut up!" Smiles

Faisal: "Lucky bastard, Harsh!"

Me: (To Faisal) "She is kidding, dude. She has a boyfriend."

Kavitha: "Huh! How sure are you, Harsh?"

Me: "You do not look single, Kavitha."

Kavitha: "Well, you definitely look single, Harsh."

Me: "Keep guessing." Winks

Kavitha: Smiles

Faisal: "Kavitha, did you know Harsh has a girlfriend who works in this same office? The real reason he joined here is because of her."

Kavitha: "Huh! Is that true? How do I not know this, Harsh? Who is she? Which batch?"

Faisal gave her the details—name, batch, and joining date. This was not the girl I mentioned in the above chapters who abandoned me. This girlfriend, let us call her SR, had been with me for four years and was my co-aspirant. The entire office heard about SR's boyfriend—me—who waited for two whole days during her interview rounds providing her with food, drinks, etc. Some in the recruitment team had seen me, but others only knew me by word of mouth.

Kavitha: "Oh! That was you, Harsh. I heard about that. SR is really lucky to have you."

Me: "Thank you, Kavitha."

Kavitha: "No problem; we can still have an ice cream as friends."

Me: "Sure, not a problem."

Faisal: "Come on, man. I need a party today."

We walked out, and then...

Faisal: "She wants your ice cream, bro!"

Me: "Asshole! Eff off man. I cannot cheat on SR."

Faisal: "Bro, you caught a big fish."

Me: "Let us forget this and go man."

When the first phase of training was completed, we transitioned to the floor to observe and gradually get involved in the process. There was immense pressure on employees to secure positive customer feedback. Those who received 5-star ratings were rewarded, and top-performing employees were recognized daily, weekly, and monthly. I thought it would be fantastic to implement a similar system at the district level in bureaucracy. It was an efficient system that reflected customer satisfaction and naturally fostered competition among employees for perks.

However, there were also significant disadvantages. Even a single negative or low rating could lead to counseling sessions for the employees. The intensity of these sessions varied depending on how lenient the trainer, SME (Subject Matter Expert), and manager were. Unfortunately, my trainer, Noela, was particularly harsh. She would publicly berate employees for receiving negative ratings, reducing some to tears and destroying their self-esteem. She failed to recognize that some people are slow learners who improve over time. Moreover, some customers were intentionally difficult and gave low ratings regardless of the service quality. Employees should not be held responsible for such external factors.

Noela's harsh treatment of one of my colleagues, named Shamitha, who ended up considering quitting, prompted me to take action. To lift her spirits, Faisal and I bought her chocolates and assured her that this job was not her entire life. That night, I posted in our WhatsApp group that human rights were being violated on the floor and that I could not work in such an environment. Noela read the message and immediately called me, but I did not answer. I texted her that I would discuss it with her the next day.

When I met with Noela, I told her I was overqualified for this job, which she took as a personal affront. She arranged a counseling session with the Floor Manager, Mr. **Saad**, who spent 15 minutes trying to convince me to retract my statement. His comparisons to school kids and threats of blacklisting did nothing to sway me. After he left, I had a direct conversation with Noela.

Confronting the Issues

Noela: "See, Harsh! You are so talented. Why do you want to take a stand for people? At the workplace, you have to be selfish and cruel. Talk for yourself. You can grow so much in this organization that you will touch the shores of New York, Sydney, and Dubai. I am enjoying all those perks from the company. Rethink your decision."

Me: "Let me tell you something, Noela. Since I am working for the Amazon client, I will tell you about Jeff Bezos' example. I heard this from a professor of mine mentioning from one of the interviews of Mr. Bezos that he wakes up early at 4 a.m. and spends four hours responding to emails from his employees, regardless of their hierarchy. This practice, known as Grapevine[5] in management parlance, reflects his belief that without his employees, Amazon is nothing."

Noela: (Silent, with a deep, helpless look)

Me: "Now tell me, is what you do with your trainees correct?"

Noela: "There are no trade unions here. I definitely don't encourage you."

Me: "Well, I can't deceive myself. This is how I am. I have no union behind me. All that I am doing is within the bounds of the law. In fact, you violated it. I want to leave for the day; I have a throat infection."

Noela: "Take permission from Saad and leave."

Me: "I'll let you know my decision by evening."

5　Jay　T　Knippen, 'Grapevine　communication:　Management　and employees' [1974] 2(1) Journal of business research 47-58.

Resignation

I texted Noela that evening about my decision to resign. I went to the office to submit my ID card and other property the next day. I quit my work, clearly stating in my resignation letter that Noela was solely responsible. Saad, in a fit of fury, fired four of my batch colleagues who had supported me. We all completed our exit formalities together.

As I was leaving, Kavitha, two other trainers, and some from the recruitment team came to bid me goodbye and wish me luck for my exams. They escorted me to the lift, offering a warm farewell.

Kavitha: "So, our ice cream treat is still pending."

Me: "Come down to Bangalore sometime." (Smiling)

Kavitha: "Definitely!" Hugs

Despite warnings from the management not to contact me, my batch mates and I remained in touch. I felt honored by their admiration. A month later, I returned to Bangalore to restart my preparation. I learned that 8-10 people, including the team leader, had left the firm within a month. Out of the 22-member batch, only 6-7 remained. Noela was eventually fired in the next 3 months by her very own manager Saad due to her rivalry with other trainers. Other batches, led by more compassionate trainers, retained their full numbers during the training period.

Reflections

This brief experience provided valuable insights into the corporate world in India. I made good friends, got a break, and learned about governance techniques that could be applied to public service, such as measuring citizen satisfaction akin to customer satisfaction. To prevent labor law violations, the bureaucracy could employ secret agents to work in corporations and ensure compliance.

I realized that I was a natural leader capable of influencing people and effecting change. Although I had to quit early due to my upcoming exam, I knew I could have fought until all demands were met. I am dedicated to public service, always striving for justice for the downtrodden. Even when those I fight for lack the courage to support the cause, I remain undeterred.

"The mind that opens up to a new idea never returns to its original size." – Albert Einstein

VI. Collapse of Ivory Tower

In Maslow's Hierarchy of Needs theory, there are five levels. I reached self-actualization at a very young age by extensively nurturing my intellectual pursuits, while others around me gradually climbed the hierarchy from physiological needs to security to social, to self-esteem. However, I lately realized that my self-actualization was unsustainable without addressing the lower needs.[6] Firstly, they were not fulfilled because of lack of proper parenting at the household and secondly, by choice, I sacrificed these needs for a higher cause. Achieving this cause could have eventually provided a solid foundation to fulfill all the lower needs effortlessly. Yet, obstacles are inevitable, challenging us to prove our potential. Despite the unsustainability of my self-actualization, it helped me face these challenges effectively. It is important to remember that regaining that stage is possible once the difficulties pass. This kind of journey is common among Indian civil service aspirants.

A day in my life as an aspirant revolved around addressing the issues humanity faces and devising progressive solutions using available resources and technology. My mornings might start with

---

[6] C AliceAnn, E Powell, et al., "Maslow's hierarchy of needs as a framework for understanding adolescent depressive symptoms over time" Journal of Child and Family Studies, 29(2) (2020) 273-281.

topics like cryosphere conservation, groundwater replenishment, or municipal solid waste bioremediation. By the next hour, I would delve into anti-defection laws or the balance between majoritarian politics and equality in a democracy, ending the day with discussions on global recession or capital account convertibility. The aspirant community typically immerses itself into serious disciplines all day round and surrounds itself with serious peers, avoiding outsiders i.e., who are not into these serious disciplines. We focus inwardly on knowledge sharing, ensuring our discussions always contribute to human progress.

In contrast, at the corporate IT firm, conversations revolved around the entertainment and sports industries, the personal lives of celebrities, religion, and superficial political complaints. Most of the day was spent on these topics alongside work. From the start, I felt isolated and was often perceived as non-interactive, non-participative, and unsociable by my colleagues. Each day added to my social awkwardness and introverted tendencies. It was not anyone's fault, nor was it a culture shock. I had been similar during my undergraduate days, distant; it could also be attributed to my autistic nature. In such social distance, I ensured my knowledge never remained stagnant; I progressed into advanced academics, which brought higher responsibilities and a deeper understanding of the world.

However, I began to realize that I was detached from the realities of the society I lived in, a condition often referred to as Ivory

Tower Syndrome.[7] This phenomenon occurs when individuals become disconnected from the ideas, cultures, lifestyles, and sentiments of the people around them. It is a common issue in bureaucracies worldwide. In elite services or higher levels of bureaucracy, personnel often develop this syndrome during their knowledge-acquiring stages. These elites are sometimes perceived as all-knowing figures or godfathers or *maibaap* who understand societal needs and believe they are the enablers of public services. This syndrome prevents them from engaging with or consulting public opinion, relying instead on recommendations from centralized surveys conducted by distant scholars. Consequently, they form a privileged and isolated class, often referred to as the SAHEB-Culture.

At lower bureaucratic levels, there is an attempt to imitate this SAHEB-Culture, adopting its traits artificially. This imitation is known as the Demonstration Effect[8] and also impacts the general public due to the insensitivity exhibited by these imitators, which is termed BABU-Culture.[9] Many governance issues stem from

---

[7] A Chantler, 'The ivory tower revisited', 37(2) (2016), Discourse 215–229.

[8] Dr Helal Uddin Ahmed, 'Impact of demonstration effect in society' (The Financial Express, 12th November 2017) <https://thefinancialexpress.com.bd/views/views/impact-of-demonstration-effect-in-society-1510155138> accessed June 2021.

[9] Ganesh R, "The Ruler vs Ruled Culture and Babudom, 29th May 2023, OpIndia <https://www.opindia.com/2023/05/babudom-modi-govt-must-drain-the-swamp-bureaucracy-here-is-why/> accessed December 2023.

this disconnection and can be resolved when this problematic nature is addressed.[10]

Here, I felt it was necessary to explain these concepts to illustrate my approach towards my colleagues. I did not want to remain trapped in the Ivory Tower Syndrome, and I was grateful for the realization I had upon joining the firm. I had previously believed that my peers, with their seemingly lower aims, were happier because they did not strive for much beyond earning a living. However, I realized that the pursuit of pleasure is a fundamental human tendency. While I sought pleasure in power and achievement to do good for the public at large, my peers found it in entertainment and simpler goals. This insight helped me understand that happiness and satisfaction can be derived from different sources, depending on individual aspirations and values. Everyone has their own unique aims based on their capacities, resources, and energies. It is essential not to judge others comparatively. Respecting each person's capabilities and the goals they set is crucial for harmonious living in society.

---

[10] Dr Sudhanshu Sarangi, "Sir, Saheb, Salute: Why India's culture of excessive reverence must go" August 25, 2017, Hindustan Times <https://www.hindustantimes.com/opinion/sir-saheb-salute-why-india-s-culture-of-excessive-reverence-must-go/story-DnTkxm84ozFfLQfkbOQtlL.html> accessed August 2020.

Low aim is a crime; have a great aim[11]

- Late Dr. A.P.J. Abdul Kalam, Hon. Ex-PoI

The above quote is debatable. The interpretation of such a statement depends on an individual's thinking capacity. For some, aspiring to become a manager in a company is a significant aim, while for me, the goal is to govern a country and be part of the elite politico-administrative class (quinary sector), regardless of which country I move to. I began to understand how the average person thinks and started admiring them for their aspirations and what they were willing to achieve in their lives.

I eventually met remarkable individuals with diverse dreams: some aspired to start their own businesses in various fields; others aimed to become motor-racing champions, renowned athletes, or models. Some were already successful fitness trainers, soft-skill trainers, and counselors. As I opened up to people, they revealed their hidden talents, such as dancing, singing, painting, and poetry. I found myself appreciating everything around me. They were all happy in their own ways—some enjoyed clubbing, while others

---

[11] At a speech to the students of St.Mary's Anglo Higher Secondary School at Kamarajar Arangam, Tamil Nadu, India on Parents' Day, August 2014

preferred concerts. Together, they formed a vibrant, composite community.

It was preposterous on my part to believe before joining here that serious disciplines are everything. When someone actually spoke of movies or sports, I was an ignorant to them just like how I felt about them when I spoke my disciplines. In no time, my ivory tower collapsed, and I became one among them—at least to a larger extent. Though my ideals and principles remained the same, my lifestyle adapted to include a broader range of experiences and perspectives.

VII. Spoils System Revisited

The spoils system is a political practice associated with any ruling government of the day. It is a concept in political science that explains how a political party that wins an election rewards its supporters, friends, family, and financial backers with administrative positions. Although the Pendleton Act, 1883[12] abolished this practice in the United States, it continues to influence third-world politics in the 21st century. Civil Services neutrality is in the conduct rules only on paper but never in practice.[13] India, for example, still suffers from this harmful political practice, which can be seen as a modern extension of feudalism. While the spoils system operates within a democracy until it is identified and eradicated, both systems share similarities in their structure and impact on society. Hence, I see spoils system as a neo-feudal mechanism and I may use the names alternatively.

Political institutions are a reflection of the society from which they emerge. Similarly, corporate management often mirrors the same feudal attitudes present in society.[14] In the Orient, especially in

---

12 Adelbert Bower, 'The first two decades of Pendleton Act: A study of civil service reform' (University Studies of University of Nebraska 1935).

13 Charles Wilby, "Municipal Reform Impossible under the Spoils System" (US National Civil Service Reform League, 1894).

14 Z H Allen, 'Appeasement and the Apocalypse: The Road to Corporate Neo-Feudalism Foretold in Atwood's Oryx and Crake', 17 (2024) Margaret Atwood Studies, 130–143.

India, both politics and companies are plagued by feudal tendencies.[15] In pre-democratic times, land was the primary transactional entity, but in the neo-feudal corporate culture, any benefit, whether in cash or kind, can be a transaction. Personal *quid pro quo* relationships are maintained, often unrelated to the firm's production activities. Self-aggrandizement takes precedence over collective profits and growth.

Sagar always told me that CF was a family business and that we were outsiders. The company was ruled arbitrarily from the top, with the Assistant Vice President (AVP) Kris acting as the feudal lord or overlord and his appointees i.e., the project managers as vassals. In the feudal system, overlords provided land to vassals, who in turn offered advice, loyalty, and military service. This quid pro quo arrangement was essential for both parties, hence symbiotic in nature. Similarly, in this neo-feudalism set up, the AVP provided projects to friends, family, and acquaintances, who then remained loyal to their patron. This practice is highly undemocratic, uncivilized, and nepotistic.

The neo-vassals scrambled like rats around a bowl of milk, misusing the company's budget to visit places like California and

---

[15] Times of India, "India's political parties have a feudal approach in a republic" (January 11th 2022) <https://timesofindia.indiatimes.com/blogs/toi-editorials/indias-political-parties-have-a-feudal-approach-in-a-republic/> accessed March 2023.

other states where clients were based. These individuals would never have had the opportunity to fly if not for their positions in the company. They admired Western lifestyles but failed to adopt and implement the practices. These neo-vassals acted as though they ruled India simply because they had the chance to visit advanced countries, and their conversations often degraded standards and values of their fellow human beings of the same level that never got chance to visit the United States. Petty! Despite their ignorance, they criticized the free-thinkers. Should I call them muggles? I believe I should stick to using the term common minds.

Only those with a democratically trained perspective can see the absurdity in their common beliefs. They fail to see the direct relationship between personal behavior and societal impact, mistakenly feeling prestigious for undeserved reasons. Ultimately, it was all a game of nepotism and money circulation amongst favorites.

Let me list the vassals of each project:

- **Shiva**, who previously earned 4 LPA at a remote company, was hired overnight as a manager for an on-site Google project at CF with a pay of 13 LPA.
- **Bharadwaj**, an assistant manager appointed overnight to Google on-site, was brought in to CF with a 12 LPA package from a minor firm where he earned 3.5 LPA.

- **Raghu** was given two US projects to handle and his packages & commissions were always clandestine.
- **Romeo** was assigned an off-site Apple project.
- **Lavanya** was given another minor off-site Apple project. Despite frequently being on leave, when she did come to the office, she spent the entire day either in the cafeteria or gossiping with the AVP and co in the conference room.

All these individuals are relatives or close associates of the AVP, Kris. When this men's club needed to recruit someone from outside, they ensured the candidate belonged to a particular social class or caste. The preferred sections of society were typically Caste-Hindus,[16] or the dominant castes like Reddy, Gowda, and Lingayat. This bias was evident in their actions, as they openly discriminated against non-dominant castes, minorities, and people from backward areas like North Karnataka. This blatant discrimination was shocking to me. This is not a baseless allegation; I would narrate the atrocities in the following chapters.

The off-site Google project had an efficient team with a very determined manager, **Pranay**, and an assistant manager, **Srikanth**. This project reported to **Manish**, the delivery team head, who was charismatic and clever. However, even this team was not free from the influence of feudal relations, as the team

---

[16] Caste-Hindus = Brahmin, Kshatriya, and Vaishya.

leaders and pod leads were loyalists to the allies. The on-site Apple project had Manish's relatives as managers. They were efficient in their work and did not oppress other teams, so no complaints could be made against them. Nonetheless, an element of nepotism permeated every nook and corner of the organization.

How did the company function?

Given the prevalence of the feudal system, one might wonder who was capable of managing the business of the firm effectively. How did projects avoid collapsing with such inefficient project managers, team leads and pod leads under the AVP? The answer lies in the existence of *serfs* as scapegoats who kept the show running. In each project, at least one Assistant Manager and one Senior Team Leader were responsible for maintaining operations effectively. These individuals were highly efficient and heavily exploited, and they, in turn, demanded the same level of output from the senior analysts and analysts. They can be compared to the bonded labor under serfdom, which comprised the poor peasantry of the vassals.

Universal Reality: The more efficient and committed one is to their work, the more exploited they become in the workplace. This is a generalizable truth with no exceptions.

Minor perks were occasionally thrown at these high performers, who were forced to stay loyal to their managers. The vassals instilled a sycophantic attitude in these workers through a carrot-and-stick approach. This was the only way to fulfill clients' requirements.

64

On a lighter note, whenever a new employee finished their joining formalities and came on board, Sagar and I would greet them with a sarcastic "Welcome to CF" followed by hearty laughter. When they asked why our welcome sounded satirical, we would tell them they would understand in time.

VIII. Maiden Counter Politics

As expected, my inevitable confrontation with Indira eventually happened. From the very first day, her behavior towards me was apathetic. Repeatedly, she told me outright that I would be a problem for the organization and frequently told Gary in my presence that hiring me was a mistake. I did not let it bother me; she was clearly trying to provoke me, and it was my business whether I chose to stay or leave; not her business. She may have correctly sensed my activist stance and predicted that I might raise issues in the company in the future, but that was irrelevant to her, once I am hired and posted.

On my first day, during a late lunch in the cafeteria, she made a snide remark about how I was eating like a "pig." I was tempted to retort, "Pigs don't use cutlery, unlike you uncivilized scum eating with bare, dirty hands," but I had to stay silent because Gary was also eating with his hands. I knew she was trying to provoke me to confirm her negative opinion. She did not stop there. During casual conversations about the country's political atmosphere, I often made mocking comments about the Indian societal setup. Indira, intending to hurt me, maliciously remarked, "Why do you blame the country for your inability to crack the civil services?" I handled her with patience each time, knowing it was futile to explain the demands of that prestigious examination to someone so foolish and ignorant. I understood her tactics and chose not to react.

Three resignations occurred in the Apple off-site project, and Sagar asked Indira to provide the names of replacements. She initially sent the names via Hangouts chat, but Sagar requested she email them instead in a formal manner. The email we received had the project name as the subject and simply said "sent" in the body, with no names or details.

Sagar (irritated): "She basically does not know how to do her job."

Me (confused): "Where did she send the names?"

Sagar (sarcastic): "She leaves it to our interpretation. She thinks Hangouts is an official onboarding confirmation."

Me: "Huh! Bloody lapdog of Gary's!"

Indira began interfering in my work. Company policy required candidates to have their education and work-related documents on hand for verification. At the start of every recruitment drive, I announced that candidates without documents should leave the interview process. Despite this, it was normal for people to lie about having their documents during the interview, only to fail to submit them later. Indira accused me of patronizing the wrong candidates and had a heated argument with me over the phone, claiming I was negligent in my duties. I wondered how I could possibly check all candidate's emails and documents during each recruitment drive. In the case of experienced profiles, some candidates presented fake experience documents, which should be the responsibility of the Background Verification Team of Core HR, not the recruitment team. Gary, for the first time since I joined, warned me without considering the facts. I was questioned about how I hired people without documents.

I discussed the matter with Sagar, who reassured me to stay confident because he knew my work and had justifications for everything. Everyone knew I was being victimized because I was new, with a voice. It was unreasonable to hold one person responsible for the mistakes of the candidates walking in.

Another strange thing happened afterward. Gary instructed that every candidate I interviewed must now go through a personal interview (PI) round with Indira. Previously, the second PI round was also conducted by the same interviewer who handled the first round before the candidates were sent to the client round. This function was now taken out of my hands. I was effectively made subordinate to Indira, despite both of us being Executives on the same level. I argued that if there were issues with my recruitment style, the reporting authority should handle the PIs, not someone of the same hierarchy. Sagar was annoyed by this development. He asked me to be patient and promised to think of a solution. Under Indira's influence, Gary began behaving strangely towards

Sagar as well. As they functioned arbitrarily, Sagar and I formed our own counter-lobby against them.

Indira was always wary of Raghu's team. She could never close the positions for their projects, creating a virtual rivalry with her. The TAG team was already weak compared to those mighty projects, and Raghu's team wantonly rejected candidates to blame TAG for our inefficiency. This led to many escalations against Indira from Raghu's projects. His entire team hated her. Fortunately, I got to work on those urgent requirements. For Raghu's positions, I never sent candidates to Indira for a second round. With Sagar's strategic guidance, I shadowed the final round of interviews to avoid unnecessary rejections. I grasped the style of Raghu's team and guided the final round candidates to crack in. I successfully closed those positions and informed Gary that it was not as complicated as Indira made it out to be. The next morning, I received congratulatory texts from Indira, but she took my success seriously and increased her harassment. She made me rework every task multiple times forcing me to stay late at the office almost every day. I was so disturbed by these events that they affected me even after I got home. I faced burn out because of harassment.

For instance, in mid-December, a series of requirements came up to fill fresher vacancies for clients like Google and Apple. We needed to fill about 40 positions within ten days. It was a stressful time, but I always aimed for a 1:3 ratio for final positions—

sending three candidates for every position to be filled. To select those three candidates, the ratio was 1:10 that I maintained. I knew my work well and had perfect planning, even under pressure. During the ten-day period, we interviewed more than 1200 candidates: 120 candidates for final round and then 40 selects as per the plan. As usual, Indira either arrived very late or did not show up at all during these mega walk-ins. Sagar and Aparna never involved themselves in weekend walk-ins unless there was a huge requirement.

The entire burden fell on me and Gary, but Sagar offered to help me as he did not want to leave me alone with Gary after the strange events that had occurred. We managed to meet the deadline and provided an adequate number of candidates for the client round, which was conducted by CF staff on-site. We finally selected 129 candidates for the final. Candidates were informed to come to the office for their PI rounds with Indira. Each day, 35-45 candidates were called in, and we completed the list in three days. However, on the third day, they were not provided with the correct address in the email, a significant oversight by Indira. All the candidates ended up at the Marathahalli office and met me there. I had to inform them that the interviews were actually being held at the Bellandur branch.

Many of the candidates came from poor backgrounds and could not afford the additional travel expenses. They had borrowed money from friends for the interview day or received limited funds from their parents, specifically planned for lunch and exact bus fare. Despite this, they made their way to the other branch. Some spent their lunch money on auto-rickshaws to avoid being late, while others ran to the other branch. When they finally arrived, Indira made them wait for a while. She called out the names of the candidates, looked their faces, and did not say a word. She sent them back without any information about the next round, instructing them to contact me for any doubts. All the candidates, in the scorching heat, walked back to Marathahalli to speak with me. They recounted, minute by minute, what had happened at Bellandur. I reviewed the selection list and found that Indira had rejected 104 out of the 129 candidates I had sent over the past three days. It was almost 2:45 PM, and none of them had eaten lunch. I could tell most of them did not have the money to get back home. They had come expecting to be moved to the final round.

I WAS OUTRAGED BY THE APATHY.

I called Indira, demanding an explanation.

Indira: "You are good for nothing. It is time to go home. You are poor at recruitment."

Me: "And?"

Indira: "When will you learn how to work? How many times do I have to tell you not to use your brain when I am here? Ask me what not to do, for god's sake!"

Me: "Alright!"

I cut the call and I apologized to the candidates and asked them for some time to resolve the issue. I assured them of justice soon and sent them back home for the day. I then went to Sagar's office and informed him about the 104 rejections without any given reason. He advised me to confront Gary directly. I called Gary and expressed my outrage over Indira's inhumane treatment of the candidates. Gary tried to reprimand me, claiming I did not know my job and could not judge people correctly.

Me: "I'm glad you said it, Gary! I am fine with it when YOU say this. But I heard the same words from Indira. She is not my reporting authority, and I do not give a damn. There will be an escalation against her. What can you do about it?"

Gary: "There seems to be a huge misunderstanding. I think you both should talk."

Me: "I already feel like I'm talking to Indira when I talk to you."

Gary: "What do you mean?"

Me: "You are repeating her words."

Gary: "You can't talk to a manager this way."

Me: "Exactly! You are a manager to both of us. Why don't you talk to her the same way you are talking to me?"

Gary: "Harsh, I spoke to her too. Whatever she did was correct."

Me: "Rejecting 104 out of 129 candidates? Am I a fool to invest my time selecting them all?"

Gary: "What?! 104 rejected? I did not know that. Wait, let me check the sheet."

Me: "Yes. These candidates were so poor they didn't have lunch and had to walk between our two branches."

Gary: "God! I'll talk to Indira."

Me: "If she has a personal grudge against me, she should take it out on me, not on the unemployed youth of the country. She cannot play with their lives. What she did today is unforgivable. She failed to maintain professionalism and acted childishly. Did you ask her how this impacts the firm's reputation? Does she understand the concept of 'word of mouth'? She brought disgrace to CF's TAG in the market today. What is the solution? I can't take this from her anymore."

Gary: "What solution do you want?"

Me: "Increase the team size and clearly demarcate the work. No two people should be working on the same requirement. We need a division of labor in the team."

Gary: "I'll come to that branch. Let us discuss. We need to talk to Kris to get approval for increasing the team size. I'll take care of that soon."

Me: "Thank you."

I could not forget the difficulties faced by the candidates. It was a serious issue affecting the firm's reputation. There was no action from Gary, as always. On January 3, 2019, I decided to escalate the matter. I sent an email to Sagar and asked him to forward it to the AVP. Sagar suggested that I also lobby with project managers who had issues with Indira. A series of escalations hit Kris's inbox from selected individuals. Here is my email:

Hi Kris

Subject*: An Escalation Against Harassment*

This is to write to keep you informed about the difficulty I am facing with Indira

-TAG team. I would like to pen down each deed of her against me in the span of my employment. I surely believe I am in good rapport with the managers and team leads of all the projects

including on-site panel members. I cannot understand why only Indira has issues with me as below:

Bullying Behavior: *I am meted out with an inhuman treatment at Indira's hands*

a. From the day I joined, Indira has repeatedly insinuated that I would be detrimental to the organization due to my involvement in various civic activities. Despite my reassurances of long-term commitment, she has persistently questioned my suitability for the role. On multiple occasions, she has openly expressed to my manager, Gary, her belief that recruiting someone like me was a mistake, citing unfounded reasons such as my resume being "fluctuating." This unwarranted criticism has been deeply offensive and demoralizing. While I initially attributed her behavior to probationary scrutiny, the constant negativity has taken a toll on my mental and emotional well-being. It is unreasonable to expect me to endure such bullying, especially considering that I underwent thorough evaluation by the Assistant Vice-President prior to my selection. Indira's continued skepticism about my selection reflects poorly on the judgment of higher management. Furthermore, her fixation on my past activities, despite them being open for background verification, is baseless and unjustified.

b. I have been subjected to offensive and sarcastic inquiries from Indira about my commitment to the organization, delivered in a derogatory tone. Despite responding generously to each query, I have struggled to comprehend the underlying motive behind her questioning, which has become increasingly apparent in recent times.

c. Indira's use of uncivilized language during conversations has been deeply unsettling. On numerous occasions, I have regretted not documenting our interactions, particularly when she made derogatory comments in the presence of Gary. For instance, on my first day at the office cafeteria, I was taken aback by her insensitive remarks, leaving me at a loss for an appropriate response. Gary's silence on such occasions has compounded my distress.

Inappropriate Guidance*: There has been a lack of proper process knowledge sharing and instances of intentional misguidance. This is not merely an accusation but a fact I can substantiate with specific instances.*

   a.   Initially, I was instructed to allow candidates to use the internet during their tests, despite raising concerns about surveillance. I was assured it would not pose an issue. However, after the evaluation, the client reported instances of content copying. I was unfairly accused by Indira of facilitating malpractice, despite strictly adhering to the instructions. Accepting blame was my only recourse, given my position in the hierarchy. This incident amounted to victimization.

b.   *During my first week, I received no orientation about our organization's processes or projects. Despite this, I was immediately tasked with conducting numerous interviews. Indira continuously criticized my candidate selections without providing any guidance or training. It was only when Gary and Sagar stepped in to train me, due to Indira's neglect, that I began to grasp my responsibilities. Despite seeking guidance from them, Indira persisted in her baseless criticisms, which amounted to harassment. As a newcomer, I expected proper guidance on our processes and project introductions.*

c.   *I have endured ongoing subjugation under Indira's authority, despite her not being my reporting manager. My contributions as a team member are met with verbal abuse, exemplified by her instructing me not to engage my intellect in scheduling candidates. Moreover, I am required to seek her approval for scheduling, even though it falls outside her recruitment purview. The lack of information about halted recruitment processes adds to my frustration and sense of helplessness. I have promptly reported these issues to my reporting authority, as Indira's attempts to assert control over me are unacceptable.*

***Sadistic Subjugation**: I am started to be treated as a slave. When my performance is perfectly in place, I am astonished to know why I am being troubled.*

a. I find myself increasingly subjected to treatment resembling enslavement. Despite maintaining optimal performance, I am bewildered by the unnecessary challenges I face. For instance, Indira refuses to acknowledge responsibility for candidates I have shortlisted. She informed the joining-formality team that she would not interfere with the approval and onboarding process for candidates I recommended. However, it is crucial to recognize that all candidates sourced by the TAG team belong to CF. Indira's failure to grasp this basic concept reflects an illogical and absurd approach. It is disheartening to witness such feudal mentalities and self-aggrandizing behavior within the team, which undermines unity and tarnishes the company's reputation.

b. Out of the 129 candidates I provided to Indira for the December flash requirement, she rejected 104 outright. Many candidates returned disheartened, having not undergone interviews. This pattern indicates deeper issues. Reflecting personal grudges in the work environment is unacceptable and must be addressed immediately to prevent further damage to CF's reputation.

c. Despite being well-trained, I find my ability to independently manage the recruitment process compromised by negative influences, particularly Indira's harassment. While I am supervised and guided to efficiently fill vacancies, Indira's behavior hampers our team's effectiveness and adds unnecessary complexity to our hiring process. Multiplicity of command is prevalent in the team.

d. Indira consistently avoids handling freshers' walk-ins on weekends, leaving the team to shoulder the pressure alone on non-working days.

e. I am often treated as immature, rather than an independent professional, leading to reprimands from managers due to Indira's inappropriate communication. For instance, innocuous tasks like sharing feedback with candidates are misrepresented, leading to unnecessary conflicts and misunderstandings.

f. Indira frequently dumps candidates into various processes at Marathahalli without prior notification, causing chaos for project managers and team members alike.

g. Constant nitpicking over trivial matters wastes valuable team time and undermines productivity. For example, blaming me when candidates are uninformed about certain details overlooks the possibility of genuine oversight or late arrivals. These distractions make it challenging to focus on essential tasks.

The concept of "Self-Fulfilling Prophecy" in psychology offers a poignant illustration: Imagine an individual from a specific religious community repeatedly labeled as a terrorist solely based on their faith. Eventually, this person may feel compelled to defend themselves forcefully, only to have their defensive actions misconstrued as terrorism, thus perpetuating the original allegation. Similarly, I find myself unjustly targeted by Indira, incessantly labeled as a problem for the organization. It seems she awaits the moment when I react, fulfilling her unfounded prediction. However, Indira lacks the authority to supervise me as if she were my reporting manager, resorting to these manipulative tactics that detrimentally impact team productivity and tarnish the organization's reputation.

I feel harassed by Indira's attitude every minute, causing immense stress and hindrance that impairs our team's long-term performance. Despite meticulously documented and pre-planned performance, courtesy of my thorough training, I am unjustly portrayed as a problem by Indira. However, I maintain positive relationships with managers, team leads, and colleagues, demonstrating my commitment and professionalism. Yet, enduring constant criticism from Indira is tormenting and traumatic, creating a hostile work environment that is unsustainable.

I implore for a resolution mechanism to address this ongoing conflict amicably. I am willing to handle any workload pressure, often staying late, working holidays, or remotely. However, I cannot endure harassment any longer. It drains me physically and emotionally. I hope for prompt action to alleviate this situation.

On January 8th, 2019, Indira was terminated effective immediate. Her abrupt redundancy brought a mix of reactions across the office. Sagar, Pranay, Srikanth, and I found ourselves celebrating the news, relieved by the resolution to the ongoing issues. However, Gary's explanation of Indira's departure raised eyebrows. His attempt to portray it as a voluntary resignation seemed dubious to us. We were not naive enough to believe that someone leaving voluntarily would bypass the mandatory two-month notice period. It was clear that both Indira and Gary had made a mockery of themselves.

Curious about the sudden turn of events, I confronted Gary:

Me: "When did this happen, Gary?"

Gary: "Last evening, Harsh!"

Me: "Why the sudden departure?"

Gary: "She had some personal problems."

Me: "Oh! That is unfortunate. Shouldn't we have organized a farewell for her?"

Gary: "She was not in the mood."

I realized it was time to take action against the predator in our midst. The relentless harassment had pushed me to my limits, compelling me to resort to drastic measures. As Gary sat alone in his office after Indira's exit, I seized the opportunity to rally her detractors and initiate a countermove. This marked my first successful foray into office politics.

IX. Con Artists

Contemporary leadership theories in management criticize counterproductive leaders in the corporate world. These leaders negatively impact subordinate performance, yet they continue to rise and dominate. How is that possible? They employ survival tactics such as ideology, bureaucratic pathology, and dramaturgy.

- **"Ideology:** Preaching values but never practice.
- **Bureapathology:** Insisting on subordinates following their decisions without any democratic input.
- **Dramaturgy:** Project confidence even when their internal traits are not genuine."[17]

As per Victor Thompson, individuals who employ these survival tactics are often referred to as con-artists. Their true personalities differ from their outward behavior, which they craft to appear exceptional.

For example, Raghu often preached about Western lifestyle and civic sense, but failed to practice what he preached. Some instances include:

1. **Respecting Others:** Despite advocating respect for others, Raghu had a stubborn character. I see him as a

---

[17] S Poli Naidu, 'Public Administration: Concepts And Theories' (1st edn, New Age International 1996).

personification of South Asian patriarchy. He would walk through entryways without considering who was behind or beside him. He never held doors open for women, instead, he would open and close doors abruptly, showing a lack of common courtesy.

2. **Bro-Code:** He ignored common social norms, such as maintaining distance in public restrooms. Even when the entire row of urinals was vacant, he would choose the one right next to another person, making them uncomfortable.

Such individuals regardless of how much they travel, they fail to learn from different cultures. I have encountered many people who, despite their global travels, do not respect or accept other cultures. True acceptance and respect come from living, learning, and working with people from diverse backgrounds, not just from visiting foreign lands for recreation, especially with company's money.

Educational initiatives can help broaden mindsets. For example, schools like Jawahar Navodaya facilitate student exchanges between states for a year or two. Many business and law schools include international education in their curricula, aiming to open minds and promote cultural integration. Such experiences are vital for genuine leadership development.

Dressing up well does not equate to an open mind, and a firm handshake does not necessarily mean confidence & dignity.

Without open-mindedness, work cultures remain conservative and narrow. Let me illustrate a xenophobic culture that existed in our firm.

Gary approved additional manpower for the TAG team. We advertised the vacancies, and several candidates attended the walk-in interviews. I conducted preliminary interviews with about 20 people, and Sagar shortlisted four candidates: Cathie, Rishitha, Harshitha, and another individual. Had the decision been solely TAG's, we would have extended offers. However, the AVP-Kris intervened in the selection process.

Two candidates, Cathie, and Harshitha, were clearly suitable based on their skills and knowledge in recruitment. Cathie held both a bachelor's and a master's degree in international business from Mt. Caramel, a tier-I institution and aimed to move to Canada after gaining two years of experience. Harshitha had two years of recruitment experience despite her technical educational background. Kris conducted the final interviews and surprisingly selected Rishitha and Harshitha.

Cathie's rejection was shocking because she had exceptional analytical skills, high communication abilities, and superior problem-solving capabilities. Rishitha's selection was equally surprising. She lacked an MBA or management degree, had a technical background, and only one year of experience in a technical field, though she was interested in recruitment.

We sensed something was amiss and asked Gary to get feedback sheet from Kris. By evening, we received the feedback sheet. The comment about Cathie read, "TOO FORWARD FOR THE POSITION." This response was disheartening.

Sagar: "Harsh! Welcome to CF!"

Me: "This is unbelievable, Sagar. She is a gem!"

Sagar: "Life throws unexpected turns. You have to toughen up."

Me: "F off! Come on! I am serious. She was perfect for the role given her education and expertise. What does "too forward" even mean?"

Sagar: "Maybe Kris did not understand anything she said."

Me: "She had an outstanding personality. I wish she had joined our team."

Sagar: "They probably did not want another Harsh on the team. Do you see the strategy?"

Me: "She did sound like me, of course, given her plan to move to Canada in 2-3 years, her interests including French language learning, and so on. She definitely committed a mistake by sharing her future plans with someone as parochial as Kris."

Sagar: *smiles*

This experience showed me that despite appearances and qualifications, biases can significantly impact decision-making in corporate environments. Open-mindedness and genuine evaluation based on merit are essential for fostering a truly inclusive and progressive workplace.

I met Harshitha again after the interview day during another walk-in recruitment event. She was on-boarded and started her very first week in fresher recruitment. It was just the two of us managing the entire process that day. As we chatted casually to get to know each other better, I asked her about Cathie since they had all attended the interview with Kris together.

Harshitha: "Oh! The girl who came in minis!"

Me: "I do not know what she wore, but what happened?"

Harshitha: "Why? What happened?"

Me: "She was rejected, and there was a strange comment in the feedback sheet."

Harshitha: "Really? What was it?"

Me: ""*Too forward*." Now I get it."

I could clearly see the narrow-mindedness of Kris and his allies reflected in their cheap managerial style. Kris was threatened by

Cathie's boldness. **What kind of man feels intimidated by an intelligent and confident woman**? Cathie had an urban demeanor and dress sense, which Kris might never have encountered before. He was probably unsettled by her confidence and might have even stammered or been speechless during the interview. This reaction revealed his inferiority complex and masculine ego. I realized Kris embodied patriarchy and misogyny. Such traits are common among people from certain backgrounds and those leading narrow-minded lives.

The qualities they sought in candidates were:

1. Their personal and professional lives had to fit within the "understandable cultural zone" of the higher management.
2. An obedient and "Yes-Manager" attitude.
3. Empowered behavior and a questioning tone were to be immediately suppressed.

Another observation that instantly made me lose respect for Kris was his selection of Rishitha and Harshitha, who happen to be sharing similar family background as his vassals. They were from the Reddy community, while Cathie was a Catholic whose mother tongue was English. This blatant favoritism to his own tribe was inward-looking and highly unprofessional, especially for someone heading a global firm.

Nobody Is Anybody's

In this small world of spoils entity, everyone pretended to admire those around them. Exploitation and oppression were silently endured without complaints, with any frustrations vented through gossip. Rumors and slander spread like wildfire across the office floor. Backstabbing and malicious talk were common, leaving no room for genuine conversation or personal growth. It was a miniature reflection of Indian society, filled with idle time and toxic behavior. Unlike public political life, where actions are visible, the corporate world thrived on behind-the-back accusations and rumors. In such a place, nobody truly supports anyone else. Con-artists lurked everywhere.

X. Corruption Unnoticed

In India, many corporate employees detest politics primarily due to corruption. Corruption is often more visible in public organizations because it is reported and impacts lives. However, corruption is equally prevalent in private organizations. In fact, corruption in public organizations often involves collusion with private individuals or firms to get things done. But that is another story.

Corruption is not just about bribery, which is merely one of the 40 forms of corruption mentioned in the Arthashastra by Kautilya/Chanakya.[18] Any deviant thought against morality is a corrupt thought, and any deviant action against ethics is a corrupt act. To me, corruption means desiring what is not mine. Taking a white paper from the office for personal use is corruption. If the gas cylinder delivery person demands extra money for delivery, that's unauthorized income over their salary. If a shopkeeper charges extra for cooling a beverage, that violates the Maximum Retail Price, which includes all taxes. This is all corruption. Yet, the public often ignore corruption in private settings but raise issues when a government clerk asks for an extra 500 rupees for a death/marriage certificate or a Sub-Registrar asks for 2,000 rupees for an Encumbrance Certificate. Government corruption is often

---

[18] Dr. Kuldeep Fadia and Prof. B.L. Fadia, 'Indian Administration' (Edn 2018, Sahitya Bhavan, 2018).

influenced by corporate interests, as seen in scandals like the 2G spectrum, Kargil coffin scam, and coal scam. Corruption is everywhere and must be identified and questioned.

At CF, corruption was rampant daily, often considered a "grey" area. Distinguishing between grey and black corruption is as dangerous as differentiating between good and bad terrorism. Competitors like FF offered freshers around 17,000 rupees per month, while CF paid only 11,000 rupees for the same roles. If the clients and requirements were identical, the pay should have been the same. This discrepancy suggested manipulated payroll or false accounting. As an executive in the recruitment team, I did not have access to the Service Level Agreement (SLA) between the client and the vendor. The delivery and production teams arbitrarily set the pay for beginners, and the entire pressure was on TAG to close positions. Despite knowing this, Gary never questioned it fiercely. For high-skilled positions, FF provided tough competition with a larger team, although the pay scales were similar.

Additionally, Background Verification (BGV) was only conducted for candidates in billable areas, not for those in non-billable roles or internal support staff, leading to significant risks for the firm. The budget for TAG was negligible, forcing us to join other teams to participate in events like Secret Santa, badminton, or singing. Despite being the top revenue-generating team, TAG had no funds for team activities which was absurd.

During my tenure, we had no team outings or lunches, while the core HR and business HR teams went out frequently, which was infuriating. Gary remained silent whenever asked about team activities. I once overheard that our off-site trip to Noida and Jaipur was canceled, and the budget was diverted to manufacture CF bags for that year. There were about 8-10 missing bags, which Kris claimed he gave to clients and important delegates, but even his favorite managers did not receive them. The close associates of Kris once held an informal meeting in the corridors and loudly started to blame one another for misallocating the bags; they were promised bags in the next budget round. Let us ask Birbal, to know whose hands had no oil!

XI. Annual Event

The annual day event was approaching, and a circular went out across CF Bangalore around February 15th, announcing it would be held on March 3rd. It was known for being celebrated with great pomp and show each year, and many employees were excitedly forming groups for cultural activities like singing, dancing, and drama shows.

My team, however, consisted mostly of older members: Sagar was 38, Gary was 40, and Aparna was 33. None of them were interested in joining me for the dance performance. The new team members, Rishitha and Harshitha were scheduled to join on March 1st, so I did not have anyone from my team to perform with. Despite this, I expressed my interest in participating in the dance. I had danced regularly in my early school years, but after moving to a new school in high school where no events were ever conducted, I lost the opportunity and, eventually, the enthusiasm. I saw this event at CF as a chance to rekindle my passion for dance.

I asked Sagar to help me get involved, and he spoke to an off-site Apple team who welcomed me into their dance group. I told them I had lost touch with dancing and needed guidance, and they graciously accepted me.

The dance practice began with a group of twenty, performing in ten pairs. The theme for the party was Retro, so we selected classic old songs and created a long dance sequence combining six to seven songs. The practice sessions were memorable, though I could not fully integrate into the group as they were cautious around me since I was in HR. Sagar, being a well-known and amiable senior, often visited our practice room to chat with everyone.

Balancing work and dance practice was fun. The employees' shifts were divided into two halves: morning (6 AM – 3 PM) and evening (3 PM – 12 AM). Our dance group had participants from both shifts, I practiced post-lunch with the morning shift and post-dinner with the evening shift.

Besides the dance, the group also prepared a skit about Indian soldiers dying in a war. I did not take part in the skit because I felt it was a clichéd way of showing patriotism, similar to how they decorated the office with freedom fighters' pictures for Republic Day, mistaking it for Independence Day. When I asked about the meaning of Republic Day, no one could explain it, and they looked at me as if I were anti-national. I pity at their mediocre lives!

During the skit practice, I found myself daydreaming about being public servant, missing the preparation times. I felt a pang of guilt for giving up on my dreams, especially since I still had three more attempts to pursue them.

During this period, my annual biological clock reminded me of the upcoming civil services exam, as it did every year when the notification was released, prompting me to intensify my preparation. However, I knew I was not going to apply or appear for the exam that year because I had not prepared. Despite this, a heavy ethical dilemma weighed on my mind, making me question whether I was in the right place doing the right thing.

Like my brother says, I started to feel like a swan among a flock of crows. There is no job as powerful and sought-after as the Indian civil service, with its everyday challenges and problem-solving opportunities. Having a reformatory mindset, it is not easy to survive among mediocre minds. Yet, in reality, I was sick, depressed, and exhausted from my previous attempts.

Although I had not applied for the exam, I began carrying my books to the office. I recalled KP sir's words about getting bored in a routine corporate job with no scope for creativity. So, I started arriving at the office at 6:30 AM to study for 2-2.5 hours before beginning my workday. I continued my work and stayed until midnight for dance practice, covering both shifts. After a week of this routine, I felt like I was wasting my time in the job. I felt overqualified, believing that anyone with a mere business degree could do this job. With my advanced studies beyond a business degree, I was convinced I was in the wrong place.

I believed I should be part of the state machinery, contributing to nation-building. Instead, I found myself working at a place where I had to invest my own money for my mobile bills and food on holidays, feeling underpaid for my potential. On February 23rd, I called Gary and requested a 10-day leave, which he granted immediately since I had worked through 14 holidays since joining. This leave was meant for introspection and focusing on higher studies that match my higher order skills. However, 2019 being the year of the general election, I felt devastated for not being able to participate in the state machinery as I had planned.

From February 25th to March 7th, I intended to stay away from work but found it impossible due to team shortages. I conducted interviews from home via video calls and went to the office for dance practice on alternate nights. Despite feeling overqualified and misplaced, I remained committed to my responsibilities while grappling with my internal conflict.

I was appreciated by almost everybody including the project heads for my dedication because I attended the practice even during my leave, while also managing my work from home during the leave. Sagar stayed at the office until midnight, just like me. He always encouraged me whenever I felt stuck in the past, whether it was about my failures in the civil services exams or in my love life.

One afternoon, while I was at the bank, Gary called to inform me that Kris wanted to have a word with me urgently. I went to the office to meet him and found all his allies there as well. Kris warmly received me and gave me a CF bag. He also wanted me to join the discussion group for the party's event planning. Manish and Raghu were leading the planning.

Manish suggested ordering party spectacles for everyone to wear and take selfies with. (which were exactly as in the below picture)

Picture Courtesy: Google

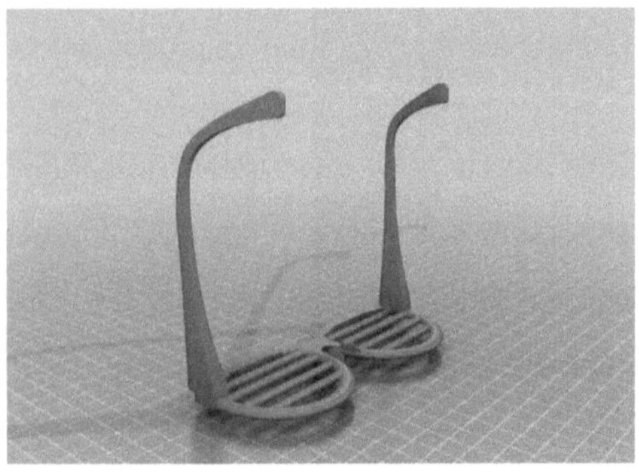

Raghu enthusiastically agreed, "They look cool! Everyone will love them for selfies!"

I voiced my concern, "Why generate so much plastic waste? It is a wasteful expenditure. No one will wear them throughout the party; they will just be strewn everywhere. Let us give out hats instead. They fit the budget and can be taken home to be used multiple times."

Manish, frustrated, left the room, saying, "Huh! This guy again! Someone talk to him! First, it was leave rotation for the projects, and now this."

Raghu sided with Manish, "No, Manish was right, Harsh. These spectacles will work better."

I conceded, "Alright."

I walked out of the conference hall and thanked Kris for the bag. I never stay where my presence is not valued. The party proceeded as they had planned.

The venue was White Orchid Convention Center at Manyata Tech Park, near Hebbal. The HR teams had to use their own vehicles, while transport was arranged for others. I arrived before 1 PM, and after lunch, we had our final dance practice on the real stage with the actual music setup. Performing there gave us all goosebumps. We literally rocked the stage; in fact we knew the stage was faulty only after our practice performance; it was given additional support from beneath before the main event took off.

The program started as scheduled. Sagar and Gary arrived late, making a courteous appearance. I was the only one from the TAG team cheering and whistling when the recruitment team received an award for our successful functioning. The chief guest was a rising comedian in the Sandalwood industry. Our final dance performance was outstanding, though the later events felt dull and the crowd turnout was disappointing.

Before leaving, Kris, Gary, Sagar, and Raghu praised my workaholic nature. Despite the event's shortcomings, the recognition made me feel special. I met all the managers from the on-site clients, whom I had never met in person despite working with them concurrently. Although I knew my exploitation would likely increase, the acknowledgment in front of the entire CF workforce made my day.

XII. Office Romance

No, not the new girls in my team, but from the Core HR verticals. On my second day at the Bellandur branch, while waiting to complete my joining formalities, a beautiful lady walked into the cabin. Her grace eventually led me into an addictive fling with her.

Her elegant walk,

Her mischief-gushing eyes,

Her captivating smile,

Her mesmerizing charm,

Made me look in awe

I stood up to offer her my chair, accidentally hitting a chair behind me with my toes. She gave me a bemused look, and an awkward silence followed as she took her seat. We introduced ourselves; her name was **Bhavana**. She looked bored as I read through the lengthy document. After the formalities, I went downstairs to work.

When I moved to the Marathahalli branch, Bhavana often visited with her teammate, **Harry**, to distribute ID cards, T-shirts, or bags to the newbies. It was their weekly routine. The three of us quickly became close. Bhavana was from Mangalore and Harry from Mysore. Bhavana was already very close to Sagar. Whenever Sagar was upset with work or office politics, his first call went to Bhavana. Even when he got drunk, he called her to vent about Gary, Kris, or Manish. Since Sagar and I had a fantastic rapport, I gradually grew closer to her.

During our first long conversation at the office, Bhavana, Harry, and I shared our past experiences, hobbies, and education. When Bhavana learned about my writing hobby and that I had authored three books, she asked me to write at least one paragraph in one of them for her. I promised her a chapter if I ever decided to write a book about my experience at CF. She was thrilled. Harry, a great chatterbox, was always hunting for girls around the floor. He was more of a people's person, and everyone liked him.

One day in December, I was in a serious mood at my bay in Marathahalli. Sagar and Bhavana were sitting next to me, sharing emotional content from their personal lives to each other. I kept silent, working on my own issues with Indira's taunts and torture. Out of nowhere, Sagar landed a kiss on Bhavana's cheek. I quickly looked around to see if anyone saw, but no one was there. When they started getting into a private moment, I stood up to respect their privacy. They snapped back to reality upon seeing me leave and returned to their respective work on their laptops. I did not say a word; I do not show curiosity in others' private lives unless they bring it up to me. They could be friends with benefits, which was none of my business. When I returned to my seat, things continued as they were.

Sagar: "Harsh! I am considering bringing Bhavana onto our team. What do you think?"

Me (unintentionally very loud): "NOOOOOOO, Sagar!"

A stunned silence spread across the floor at my unexpectedly loud response.

Bhavana (looking puzzled): "What is going on, Sagar?"

Sagar (in shock): "Harsh, what is wrong? Is everything okay?"

Me: "Look, I am sorry! Let us talk about it later, Sagar."

Bhavana left the place, and Harry followed, clearly perplexed by my strong reaction to what seemed like a minor decision. Sagar approached me that evening, curious about my outburst.

Me: "I have noticed Gary and Indira irrationally isolating other team members for their own interests. I do not want that to happen here. Once Bhavana joins our team, you both might do the same to me, just like Gary and Indira."

Sagar: "That is silly. Just because they acted that way does not mean we will. Not everyone is like them, right, Harsh?"

Me: "Fine then, if Bhavana is coming here, and I will move to her place, into Core HR. Discuss it with Gary and let me know. I am ready to shift."

Sagar: "Harry is also requesting a move to TAG. Let us see how it works out."

Me: "Did Bhavana feel bad about my reaction?"

Sagar: "Forget about that. You seemed really serious and not in a good mood."

Me: "Please convey my apologies to her."

Sagar (with a wicked smile): "You can do that too, by the way!"

Me: "Fine."

Later that weekend, after a walk-in drive at the office, I went to a club. After some drinks and dinner, I felt like calling Bhavana. I called her up and asked what she was up to. She said she had just returned from a friend's place. I told her I was coming to pick her up, and she agreed to wait. Driving after drinking was a bad habit of mine. Despite my education, I struggled to overcome it. I criticize Salman Khan for his felony but hypocritically, I did the same many times. But I always made sure I was sober enough to drive safely; not a rational excuse though. I reached Bhavana's hostel, and she emerged wearing a hot red sleeveless top with regular makeup and loose hair. Damn! I do not remember what I wore that day but I remember her attire. She looked stunning. We greeted each other with a warm hug.

Me: "Look, I am really sorry about earlier. Did Sagar explain the reason for my outburst?"

Bhavana: "It is okay. Where are we headed?"

Me: "Have you had dinner?"

Bhavana: "Yes, have you?"

Me: "Yes, let me take you to a peaceful place where we can sit and watch the runway lights from the top near HAL."

Bhavana (as I drove): "Where are you coming from?"

Me: "I was at a club. Why?"

Bhavana: "You are driving fast."

Me: "Nah, I am in control. I did not drink much."

We spent about an hour at the location, indulging in light-hearted banter. We poked fun at members of senior management and jokingly cursed each other's teams. There was a playful energy between us as we teased each other, even pretending to lift each other as if to throw into a nonexistent dump below. Bhavana had a lively spirit, which helped me, as an introvert, to open up more quickly than usual. Perhaps it was the effect of the alcohol, but I found myself sharing more easily. We found chemistry between us.

On the way back to her hostel, Bhavana expressed a craving for ice cream, so we stopped and spent another hour discussing our futures and goals. While she did not have grand career aspirations beyond her bachelor's and master's in business, she had clear dreams about her ideal life partner.

Me: "So, what are you looking for in a partner?"

Bhavana: "Someone caring, who pampers me and showers me with affection."

Me: "Sounds wonderful."

Bhavana: "And you?"

Me: "Well, my list of requirements is a bit long."

Bhavana: "Care to share a few?"

Me: "I have a thing to doctors. I have always been drawn to them."

Bhavana: "Are you planning to get sick often?" laughs

Me: "Ha ha, very funny" (*satirical*)

Bhavana: "Okay, spill the beans. Why doctors?"

Me: "Oh, it is nothing serious. Let us change the subject, shall we?"

Bhavana: "Sure, let us go."

I dropped her off at the hostel and did not see her again until I visited the Bellandur branch later. It was an evening when I was elated because Indira had been fired. I wanted to see the reaction on Gary's face and enjoy the staff's happiness. Harry and I had been planning a boys' outing for a while, and this seemed like the perfect opportunity to celebrate. When Bhavana expressed disappointment at not being invited, Harry joked about her joining us.

Harry: "What is wrong? Upset about not being invited?"

Bhavana: "Obviously!"

Harry: "Take it up with the host."

Me: "Sorry, Bhavana, but this is a boys' outing. We have already been out once."

Bhavana: "Please, Harsh! I really want to join."

Me: "Well, shall we let her, Harry?"

Bhavana: "Please say yes!"

Harry: "I do not know. She tends to get a bit wild when she has had a few drinks. Not my responsibility."

Bhavana: "I promise to keep it in check. Please!"

Me: "Alright, let us go. You can join us, Bhavana."

Bhavana: "Yayyy!"

We arrived at MG Road around 8 PM and headed to a nightclub. We indulged in shots, cocktails, and drinks, discussing the dirty politics in the office. Harry shared his frustrations about the shortage of manpower in his team and the uncomfortable encounters with Kris. Our conversation eventually shifted to personal matters, with me asking questions and them sharing their stories.

Me: "What do you want to achieve soon in life?"

Bhavana and Harry (together): "To lose our virginity."

Me: "What?! I do not think either of you are virgins."

Both: "Yes! We are tired of being that."

Me: "Well, maybe you should talk to each other about it instead of telling me."

Harry: "Ew! Not with her, Harsh!"

Bhavana: "Gross! Not with him, Harsh!"

Me: "Hahaha! Go find someone on the dance floor. There are plenty of people there."

Bhavana: "Find me a boyfriend. Let us make a move."

We were high and feeling crazy. Harry stayed silent, sitting in a corner, while Bhavana and I hit the dance floor, disturbing every guy there.

Me: "Is he the one, Bhavana?"

Bhavana: "Nope"!

Me: "Take a good look! This one must be the one."

Bhavana: "No, I will let you know when I find someone I like. Let us keep moving."

Me: "Alright."

We returned to the counter after scanning the crowd, and Harry asked if Bhavana had found someone. I joked that she had poor taste. Then, I heard an announcement that the dance floor was reserved for the staff of Dr. Reddy's from 10 PM.

Me: "Doctors are coming?"

Harry: Nope! Pharmacists."

Me: "Darn it!

Bhavana: "You never told me your doctor fascination."

Me: "Let HER go!"

Bhavana: "Ooh! Her? So, that is what it is! Your ex is a doctor!"

Me: "Bhavana! Look at me! Fuck her! Forget that! Let us ask the DJ to change the song, Bhavana. I am tired of these English songs. I need something Desi/Indian."

Bhavana: "Oh! High Five! I prefer Desi to English too."

We moved hand in hand to the DJ to request Bollywood songs.

Me: "Can you switch to Bollywood, please?"

DJ: "Only after 10 PM, sir."

Bhavana: "Come on, please! We cannot wait."

DJ: "Sorry, ma'am."

I called my best friend, a school friend, to pick me up since I knew I was not in a condition to drive home. As my friends arrived,

Bhavana and Harry left. Bhavana was heavily drunk, nearly falling off the bike. Eventually, Harry managed to drop her off at her hostel. They left just as the Bollywood songs started playing. I stayed with my friends until 2 AM before they dropped me off safely at home. The celebration of Indira's oust came to an end that night, leaving me feeling free and successful.

The next day, I sent texts to everyone, thanking them for making the party a success. I also apologized to Bhavana if I had misbehaved in any way by dancing with her hand in hand on the dance floor.

Bhavana: "We are a team. Do not worry! You are overthinking it."

Me: "I know, but it is my courtesy to apologize."

Bhavana: "I do not even remember anything."

Me: "I do. Everything we said."

Bhavana: "Please forget all of it."

Me: "No way!"

Afterward, Bhavana and I started hanging out frequently, even having unplanned evening outings for dinners or ice cream, even during workdays. Interestingly, I am lactose intolerant, so she was the only one having ice cream each time, not me.

Let me share some of Bhavana's peculiar habits. She was oddly fascinated by the smell of sanitizer, often making exaggerated expressions whenever she caught a whiff of it.

Me: "You should quit your job and sign a contract with the porn industry."

Bhavana (playfully hitting me): "Shut up, Harsh!"

Me (laughing): "At least consider Indian B-grade. Your expressions are just so fantastically over-the-top."

Bhavana: "People who are not expressive cannot appreciate expressive emotions."

Almost every time we met, she would play with the key chain of my bike, a long single tiger nail-shaped object. She even jokingly put it in her mouth for extended periods, which I found quite gross.

Me: "I will get you a dildo for that. Give me back my key chain."

Bhavana (blushing and smiling): "Harsh!"

We also frequently pretended to be engaged. She had a ring on her index finger, and I often took it off to try to place it on her ring finger.

Bhavana (smiling but hesitant): "Why do you want my ring?"

Me: "Let us pretend to get engaged. Come on, give it to me."

Bhavana: "What about a ring for you?"

Me: "It is a half-engagement. You do not have to put one on me."

She was also baffled by a few of my peculiar habits. I had OCD, not just when it came to cleanliness, but also in many other aspects of life unless I was intoxicated. One evening, we went to grab a bite to eat, and even though she insisted she was not hungry, she could not resist after seeing me eat a Frankie.

Me: "Are you sure you do not want one, Bhavana?"

Bhavana: "Absolutely sure."

As I ate, she stared at me, then asked for a bite, and then another.

Me: "No! I am not sharing."

Bhavana: "Just a piece of paneer, please!"

She reached into the Frankie with her bare hands, and I could not help but cringe. I grabbed a tissue, tore off the part she touched, and threw it in the bin nearby without looking at her.

Bhavana (shocked and furious): silent looks

Me (softly): "Bhavana!"

Bhavana (holding up her hand on to her face): eyes closed

Me: "I am sorry! You know, right?"

Bhavana (softly): "Please do not talk! I am so embarrassed."

Me (gentle): "Listen! I hate hands in food. And you did not even sanitize them."

Bhavana: "Just drop me at the hostel, Harsh."

Me: "Let us resolve this and then go."

Bhavana: (shaky voice) "Do you realize how embarrassed I feel?"

Me: "I know! I am truly sorry! I feel terrible. That was instinctive. You know and see that I never touch my food without tissues, even at the cafeteria."

Bhavana: "I see why you always said I was from a small town. You treated me differently today. I deserved it."

Me (clueless): "Please, do not take everything I say so seriously."

Bhavana: "For your information, Harsh, Mangalore is not a small town. Visit sometime. I may not have studied or worked abroad, but at least I learned not to hurt others."

The whole evening was ruined by my small act, but it had a big impact. On the way back, we barely spoke.

Me: "Shit! Shit! Shit! Sorry Bhavana! Can you once get down please!"

Bhavana (in a gruesome shock imagining something big happened): gets down

Me (frenziedly pulling the backseat): "I forgot to wear the helmet."

Bhavana: "Oh gawwwd! I am speechless again."

After dropping her off, she seemed a little better, perhaps because the forgotten helmet incident lightened the mood a bit.

Bhavana: "I did not know you were so crazy."

Me: "Listen, I am really sorry if I made you feel insulted."

Bhavana (smiling): "It is okay, baby."

Me: "Did you just call me baby? Seriously? I do not understand anything right now but that is cute, though. I use 'babes,' not baby, unless it is for a girlfriend."

Bhavana: "Noted."

hugs and I headed home.

One evening during my 10-day leave, when I arrived early at the office, the dance practice was unexpectedly cancelled due to additional project work. I decided to invite Bhavana for dinner. We headed to my favorite regular lounge, The Garage, conveniently located behind my house. Whenever I visited, I usually had the whole room to myself, ensuring privacy. Over dinner, we discussed how our shared interests had brought us closer. Our musical taste leaned towards slow-rock melodies, with a strong emphasis on lyrics rather than instruments. We both shared a love for South Indian comedy and often found ourselves watching videos of our favorite comedians.

Bhavana took interest in my phone and started watching dance practice videos. She questioned why I had not invited her and Harry to participate. I explained that Sagar had indicated you would not be interested. She was furious for not having that discussion with her. We decided to call Harry to gauge his interest, and to our delight, he agreed. The three of us decided to enroll and prepare for another performance, of our own, separate from the group. Bhavana, being skilled in dance, took charge of choreographing selected songs right on the spot. As we immersed ourselves in the music, she began teaching me the nuances of expressing love, laughter, and elegance through dance, syncing our movements with the rhythm.

In the heat of the moment, our bodies drew closer, and we found ourselves dancing intimately, locked in each other's arms, our eyes speaking volumes. As the song ended, Bhavana leaned in, blinking & closing her eyes alternatively, and I instinctively pressed her against the wall, our bodies entwined. We gazed into each other's eyes; the air thick with romantic tension.

Bhavana (bashfully): "Hmm?"

Breathing into each other, about to kiss but I gently rested my forehead against hers before pulling away.

Bhavana (with a soft smile): "What happened, Harsh?"

Me (puzzled): "I am not sure. Shall we continue practicing?"

Bhavana (still smiling): "Thinking about the past again?"

Me: "Maybe"

Bhavana: (*softly*) "You should forget her. Hearing me?"

Me: (*looking to the ground & into the air*) "I know. Let us dance!"

We resumed our dance practice, and as we enjoyed our meal, we listened to some of my singing recordings. Later, after dropping Bhavana at the hostel, I delved into the work awaiting me on the laptop, provided earlier by Kris.

The following day, Harry and Bhavana sought permission from their team manager, **Mohini**, for the dance practice. Although Gary and others were informed that we would be performing, Mohini insisted they finish their work for the day before attending practice, not permitting them to take time from working hours. I felt fortunate to have a more flexible manager, allowing me to manage my work schedule, in this regard.

Despite our excitement, we had to cancel our trio's performance due to unavoidable reasons. Finally, after much anticipation, we embarked on our shopping trip for retro costumes (theme for the ceremony) on the evening of March 2nd. While Bhavana remained undecided, I harbored a unique idea for my outfit, keeping it a secret until the last moment. However, we both agreed to wear black attire (first reason being, we both like black, second being, we met for the first time wearing black shirts at the office during my joining formality). At the Brand Factory, Bhavana tried on various funny costumes in pursuit of a retro look, but nothing seemed to click. Amidst her shopping antics, we shared lighthearted banter, and upon leaving the store, Bhavana playfully insisted on being given priority, not out of anger but to bask in the attention and affection.

Once we stepped out of the store, Bhavana decided to playfully assert herself, not out of irritation but to revel in the attention and affection. She stood her ground, demanding to be placed on the bike.

Me: "Alright, hop on, ma'am!"

Bhavana: "No, lift me and put me on the bike."

Me: "What?!"

Bhavana: "Fine, I will just stand here all night then."

With the center stand in place, I lifted her onto the back seat.

Bhavana: "Get me an ice cream."

Me: "We will get it once we find a dress for you."

Bhavana: "No, I want to eat it right here."

Me: "Ahh, Bhavana, fine, wait!"

Bhavana: "You know my flavor!"

Me: (*stressful*) "Of course, goddess!"

After fetching her dark chocolate ice cream, I asked if we were ready to leave.

Bhavana: "Let me finish this."

Me: "Why don't you just kill me?"

Bhavana: "I wish!"

Deciding to find her the perfect dress, I took her to Pantaloons. Despite the late hour, I managed to persuade the staff to allow us a few minutes to shop. While she tried on different outfits, I spotted a polka dotted skirt (white on black) that I knew she would love. However, it was the wrong size. I quickly sought assistance from the store management to alter it, and they accommodated our request, ensuring it fit her perfectly.

Me: "What about my costumes? The party's tomorrow."

Bhavana: "We will go tomorrow morning. Tell me what you need, and I will take you to a place where you will find all the male Retro costumes."

Me: "We will have to start early tomorrow."

Though I appreciated her help, I took it upon myself to buy some items the next morning before meeting her. After purchasing a red bow, black shirt, hat, and black waistcoat, I only needed suspenders. I messaged her about it, and she was thrilled, anticipating a memorable and hilarious outfit. She guided me to a men's store at the White Field Inorbit mall, where I found the perfect suspenders. Excitedly, I showed her my purchases, and she eagerly anticipated taking photos in our matching black attire. Thanks to it being a Saturday with light traffic, we arrived at the Orchid Convention Center in just an hour.

The lunch at the party left much to be desired, leaving Harry, Bhavana, and me ravenous. So, we decided to hit up a nearby KFC for something more satisfying. Surprisingly, Bhavana offered to treat us that day, a departure from her usual frugality. While waiting in line:

Harry: "Is it doomsday?"

Me: "Seriously! Bhavana is spending a penny."

Bhavana (nestling against me with a smile): "Will you two quit it?"

Harry (sarcastically): "What is with this newfound generosity? How long will this affection last?" (gesturing at our closeness)

Bhavana: "He is different from you. He cares about me."

Me: "Bhavana, you do not have to compare. We are all a team, and you are the cheerleader."

Harry (chuckling): "High five, Harsh!"

Bhavana (playing coy): "Even you, Harsh?"

Me: "Poor Bhavana!"

Harry: (*to Bhavana*) "The moment he stops caring, you will come back to me crying. Remember that."

Me: "That is for sure. But do not worry, things are crystal clear between us."

Bhavana (giving a stern look and heading to the table): "Of course."

Once back at the convention center, I had to change into my dance costume and participate in other activities before the show. I was pleasantly surprised by my own performance, which received rave reviews. Following my act, Harry wowed everyone with a surprise performance, leaving us all impressed.

Harry: "Wondering why I arrived so early?"

Me: "Impressive. I appreciate the dedication."

Afterward, I appeared in my retro attire, surprising Harry with mine & Bhavana's coordinated outfits.

Harry: "When did you guys go shopping? Why didn't you call me?"

Me: "We went late last night and this morning. This madam here was so indecisive."

Bhavana: "Hey! You never took me to the right places like I took you to Inorbit Whitefield."

Me: "I made my own arrangements, okay?"

Bhavana: "Take out those suspenders and hand them over now."

Me: "No, no. I know you are a sweetheart!"

As the performances, award ceremonies, and speeches concluded, the DJ took over. Each person was entitled to two alcoholic beverages, leading to a scramble for tokens among the teetotalers and the imbibers. Me, Harry, and Bhavana stuck together until dinner, waiting for the rest of the HR team to join us, to no avail. As we started on the starters, Harry disappeared momentarily to pick up Harshitha, a newbie from TAG who had already become close to him. Bhavana teased Harry about it in front of Gary and Sagar, and when they returned, there was a palpable spark between them.

The atmosphere grew livelier as people hit the dance floor. We finished our starters and were about to move on to beverages when Bhavana abruptly left with a guy named **Manoj** who complimented her. Manoj happened to be from same town as Bhavana, Mangalore. Feeling left out, I mingled with some onsite colleagues who praised my outfit and said I was looking cute.

An on-site beautiful lady, who was my recruit approached me.

Lady (excitement and surprise): "Harsh!"

Me (struggling to recall her name): "Hey there! Hi!"

Bhavana (from nowhere, grasping my hand forcefully): "Harsh! What the hell?" (She yanked me away from the lady)

She pulled me a few steps away, leaving me shocked and uneasy at her abrupt behavior. I felt regretful for not being able to apologize properly to the lady before leaving. I felt awkward, like an opportunity had been missed. As I stood there, a group of my other recruits, also from the on-site team, approached me.

Group: "Come sir! Join us for a dance!"

Me: "Sure thing!"

Group: "You are looking fantastic in that outfit."

Me: "Thank you so much!"

Bhavana (shouting):" Harsh, what has gotten into you? I am hungry. Go get some food for me. I will try to find an extra drink coupon for you."

Me: "Alright, guys! I will catch up with you lat"— (Bhavana interrupted, pulling me away abruptly)

I brought the food, which was placed on the table and I again went to grab a drink with the new coupon. Upon my return, I saw Manoj feeding to Bhavana, who was already tipsy. They found a spark in each other. They left to the dance floor together again and danced with great chemistry between each other. I left her there and I spent time with Harry outside the venue.

As the event wound down and vehicles began to depart, I received numerous compliments on my retro ensemble. Harry offered to drop off Harshitha, leaving me to contemplate leaving Bhavana behind, perturbed by her insincerity. When Harry returned, I expressed my frustration and asked him to drop Bhavana, but he insisted on finishing his drinks and dinner first.

Harry: "Just put her on one of the buses heading back."

Me: "Good idea." (Meanwhile, Bhavana emerged, while Manoj boarded one of the office buses since he is an employee from one of the Apple projects)

Me: "Bhavana, would you mind taking one of the buses back to the hostel?"

Bhavana: "No way! Why? These buses only go as far as the office. Others have cabs that drop them home after reaching the office. How will I get to the hostel from the office at this hour?"

Me: "Damn, that is quite a responsibility."

Harry: "It is alright, dude. Relax." (Whispers)

Me: "I am fine."

As we journeyed together, Bhavana held me close from behind, seeming unperturbed by our recent exchange. I pulled over at a flyover midway and turned to her.

Me: "I need a kiss."

Bhavana: "Right now? Here?"

Me: "Yes, here. Get down."

Bhavana: "But there are so many lights above us, and our company buses are passing by."

Me: "I do not care. It is long pending."

Despite the passing vehicles and the hoots from the buses, we shared a kiss right there, eyes closed, lost in the moment for about a minute. It was a brief respite, calming me down, yet the unresolved tension lingered. We resumed our journey, passing by the Marathahalli office, Bhavana's hostel, until we reached the Bellandur office branch. Pulling over behind the office where traffic was less frequent, I turned to her.

Me: "Do you want to go to the hostel?"

Bhavana: "No."

Me: "Then what do you want to do?"

Bhavana: "I am not sure."

Me: "How about finding a quiet spot to relax?"

Bhavana: "Your place?"

Me: "My home, you mean? "

Bhavana: "Yeah."

Me: "No. Not like this, not at this time. Look at me."

As we gazed into each other's eyes, the tension dissipated, replaced by a desire for intimacy. Our kisses grew deeper, our bodies pressing against each other, neck sucks, deep smooches and panting. Lost in the moment, we continued kissing and started to drive very slowly (about 10 km/hr) but aimlessly, our destination unknown. But our trance was abruptly interrupted by an unexpected event: a police checkpoint for drunken driving. My bike was seized by the police; dealing with the situation, I had to drop Bhavana off, the fare of the auto-rickshaw skyrocketing. As we were on the auto-rickshaw, our conversation continued.

Me: "How did this even happen?"

Bhavana: "Kris did not arrange transport for the HR teams."

Me: "Otherwise, we would be kissing on the bus, wouldn't we?"

Bhavana: "How romantic would that have been!"

Me: "Were we so lost in each other that we did not notice our surroundings?"

Bhavana (blushing and holding me tight): "Kiss me more." smiles

We kept kissing until we parted ways. Getting caught for drunk driving was an eventuality I had always dreaded, but it happened at the worst possible time. After being dropped back by the auto-rickshaw to where my vehicle had been impounded, I tried to use my connections to avoid court. Late that night, I called a senior, an IPS officer serving as an SP in the Tamil Nadu Cadre, and handed the phone to the Traffic Inspector. The inspector explained that the digital record of my blood alcohol content (BAC) had already been uploaded, leaving him powerless. However, he suggested I visit the station to settle the case out of court the next morning.

When I woke up, I realized that trying to use influence was wrong. I deserved to be caught and face the consequences. I needed counseling to ensure I never repeated this mistake. At the station, instead of settling the matter, I sought my counseling and court dates. For the first time, I felt proud of the Indian Police for upholding public safety and law. Since that night, I have never driven under the influence of alcohol. I now either book a cab or ensure a teetotaler who can drive accompanies me. This incident eradicated my bad habit of drunk driving.

Following the party, I received strange texts, pictures, and videos from colleagues about Bhavana. Some videos showed her dancing provocatively with Manoj. It did not bother me as it was consensual. She was clearly in high spirits and carefree. The texts, however, varied in tone and concern.

Person 1: "What was Bhavana doing with this guy, Harsh?"

Me: "What is wrong with that? Why are you texting me about her as if she is my girlfriend?"

P1: "Wasn't she with you?"

Me: "So! Why?"

P1: "Nothing. Give me a call, I will tell you."

P2: "Harsh! Look at Bhavana. How cheap! Isn't she such a slut? Don't you feel bad about it?"

Me: "Come on! Who are we to judge her? I have no issues."

P2: "Watch the video once. You will understand."

Me: "I have seen it. She is enjoying herself. Let us not overthink it. Why don't you judge the guy with the same mindset? Why only judge her?"

P3: "Don't you think the dance was so vulgar?"

Me: "Why don't you ask the guy to take the video off his status if it is so vulgar?"

Was I defending Bhavana from the judgmental society or from the disrepute she brought upon herself? I was not sure. What I was sure was, Bhavana lost my trust and respect for the way she treated me on the party night.

XIII. Foiled Reforms

With the annual event concluding, the entire workforce returned to their routine. I finished my leave and came back with renewed enthusiasm. With the addition of two new team members, Rishitha and Harshitha, the workload was redistributed. According to my prior agreement with Gary, no two people worked on the same requirement. I became solely responsible for experienced profiles, such as recruiting doctors, pharma professionals, dental coders, admin staff, Pod Leads, Team Leads, Versant positions, Managers, Assistant Managers, and Learning & Development Soft Skills Trainers. For the fresher roles, I guided Rishitha and coordinated with Harshitha.

The team planned to post a member from TAG at the Google client site to monitor arbitrary rejections. Sagar recommended me for this position because of my previous success with complex projects in Raghu's team. However, Gary chose Harshitha, citing her two years of experience with the client Google. I had no strong objections to this decision.

Our longstanding issues with Google began to intensify. Managers for CF, Shiva, and Bharadwaj would inform us that they would arrive within an hour, but would often show up several hours late. They never provided updates unless we called them, and their scheduled times were always inconvenient, such as 11 AM or 5 PM. If they arrived late in the morning, candidates had to wait for hours without lunch, and we often had to arrange meals from the cafeteria. When food was insufficient, candidates had to go without. If the managers arrived late in the evening, we, the recruiters, had to work beyond our hours.

This lack of consideration became increasingly frustrating. After witnessing this apathetic behavior multiple times, Sagar advised me not to stay late at the office anymore, as my efforts were being taken for granted. He suggested I refuse assignments that extended beyond a certain time. He was right. Overstaying is inefficient in theory, so I planned to complete all my work by 6 PM.

I started analyzing where my time was being wasted. The primary issue was the need to move between projects for video conference interviews without having adequate equipment. When client managers could not come to the office, they requested Video Conferences, which meant I had to stay late to return the equipment afterward. Unable to convince Gary of the need for better resources, I decided, under Sagar's direction, to write an email to higher management outlining these challenges. I had written a mail to Kris as below:

Hi Kris

Re: A request for fulfilment of dire necessity

I hope this message finds you well. I am writing to bring to your attention the urgent need for additional equipment to conduct

Pearson's Versant Tests and video conference interviews effectively.

Currently, we lack sufficient laptops and headphones necessary for these tasks. We are frequently borrowing equipment from adjacent teams, which disrupts their workflow. Even with these borrowed devices, we still do not have enough to accommodate the number of candidates taking the online tests regularly. Since each candidate requires a significant amount of time to complete these intensive tests, the borrowing teams often need their equipment back before we are finished, causing delays and inefficiencies in our recruitment process.

Additionally, our desktop PCs are not equipped with audio capabilities for video conference discussions when candidates are present in the office. The team at Marathahalli has only one laptop, which is malfunctioning.

To address these challenges and ensure a smooth recruitment process, we urgently need at least three more laptops and an adequate number of headphones. Your prompt action on this matter would greatly enhance our efficiency and effectiveness.

Thanking you in anticipation

Regards

Harsh – TAG Team

I never received a formal reply, but I did get a reaction from Gary, who was reprimanded for failing to control his team members, as I had bypassed hierarchical protocols by contacting higher management directly. Gary discussed this with me, explaining that the higher-ups preferred to hear from him as the Manager, rather than from me, an Executive. The purpose of my message was not served, and being at the lowest level in the HR hierarchy, I continued to struggle. Even Sagar could not do much to help.

There were numerous reforms needed within our organization. My studies in administration, especially by KP sir, taught me to find the good in bad situations and the bad in good ones to foster improvement. One issue I noticed was the excessive use of single-use plastic items in the cafeteria, such as cups, glasses, and spoons. I approached Kiran, an admin Executive, to suggest replacing them with biodegradable alternatives. Initially, he dismissed the idea, citing higher costs. Then, he irresponsibly and cowardly claimed it was not his concern and suggested I speak directly to the Admin Manager if I was so inclined. Sagar looked at me sympathetically, questioning with his eyes why I was involving myself in everything. Nevertheless, I sent an email to the Admin Manager, suggesting the use of Corporate Social Responsibility (CSR) funds to invest in environmentally sustainable products. Although I never received a response, over time, I noticed that plastic glasses were replaced with paper ones.

During this period, Sagar and I grew very close. He trusted me with his personal details and problems he faced at home. His aging parents required his care as his two sisters had moved abroad. Although he had opportunities to leave the country and improve his standard of living, his parents were his priority. Financial troubles due to his low salary were causing significant stress and misunderstandings at home. He often felt comfortable confiding in me, showing his tears and seeking solace. When he felt hopeless or vulnerable, he would come to my bay to sit and work with me. Together, we laughed off difficulties. We conducted interviews jointly, and I resumed scheduling a high volume of interviews each day. As I conducted the interviews, Sagar would observe the candidates.

One day, as we were interviewing, a moment highlighted the need for sensitivity and professionalism:

Sagar, gazing at a female candidate's bosoms, said, "Continue, Harsh."

I, noticing her discomfort, cleared my throat and sighed, "Sagar"

Sagar cleared his throat too, and hurriedly replied, "I'm married" in front of that candidate.

I could not control my laugh. Fortunately, the candidate also laughed it off.

After she left, I asked, "Come on Sagar! What if she files a POSH (Prevention of Sexual Harassment at the work place) complaint?"

He shrugged, "No fears, my life is ruined already."

A medical camp was organized at the office for two days. On the first day, I could not attend due to heavy work. On the second day, Sagar came to my bay, looking astonished.

Sagar: "Doctors are here. How come you did not go, Harsh?"

Me: "Are you done with the check-up?"

Sagar: "Yeah!"

Me: "What diseases were diagnosed?"

Sagar: "Cancer!"

Me: "Wait, let me go get checked."

After a while, Sagar asked me, "What about you?"

Me: "AIDS."

Sagar: "Hahahah! Call up your ex and tell her this."

Me: "Brilliant idea, Sagar!"

Meanwhile, the on-site team made our lives miserable by rejecting a large number of candidates. The local market has low educational potential. The standards of the Indian education system are such that many engineering graduates do not even know that their names should start with a capital letter. Companies recruiting these graduates need to maintain minimal skill requirements and then provide on-the-job training. Foreign companies establishing their businesses in developing countries like India cannot expect top-tier talent from the outset. They should be willing to teach practical skills to the candidates.

Sagar and I came up with an innovative idea to conduct psychometric tests to identify highly qualified candidates. We quickly implemented this test in our recruitment process.

On the other hand, the Core HR Team and the Business HR Team planned an off-site tour. However, TAG's tour was canceled, and the budget was diverted as previously stated. As a workaholic, I needed a social break. I asked Gary to arrange something for us, and we planned an outstation recruitment drive to Mysore for 3-4 days. Gary organized a trip where half a day would be dedicated to the hiring process and the rest for sightseeing. I was excited. Gary selected Sagar, Rishitha, and me to go, while Aparna and Harshitha were to stay back.

On the day we were supposed to leave, Harshitha applied for a few days' leave, stating that her grandmother had passed away. Gary was perplexed about granting more than a day off in her first month of employment. She insisted, and as a result, I was dropped from the trip to take care of the client's needs. Gary and Rishitha made video calls to share their trip experiences, and I kept telling them I was not jealous, although I was deeply envious.

Determined to make the most of my time, I decided to tackle an old, untouched requirement for dermatologists. Google needed about 20 dermatologists. I called Gary for more details, and he forwarded a one-liner description from higher management. Without a job description in place, I had no idea why Google required dermatologists! When I asked for a detailed job description, Gary said the one-liner was all he received six months ago when the requirement was first posted.

Undeterred, I collaborated with my colleague, Beulah, from one of the projects on floor, to close as many of these positions as possible. I scheduled eight interviews in one go, despite not knowing the exact requirements. I encouraged the doctors to clarify their doubts directly with the interview panel. I did that on purpose to let Shiva and Manish know how painful it is to recruit candidates without a job description. They both took this upon their ego, creating additional challenges to me.

Despite these setbacks, I remained focused on improving our processes and addressing the needs of our team and clients. Manish demanded an explanation from TAG for our actions. I emailed the delivery team, stating that TAG did not have a detailed job description (JD) for the requirement. This hurt Manish's ego, and he instructed me to communicate with my team manager to get the necessary details. I called Gary.

Me: "Can you send an email to Manish explaining that you faced the same issues as I did?"

Gary: "Honestly, I never understood that requirement, which is why I never addressed it. I am typing that now."

Me: "Great. Send the email, Gary. You are just as capable as any other manager. It is time to stand up for ourselves."

Gary: "I am so confused. What could be the consequences of this?"

Me: "Is TAG subordinate to the delivery team in any way, Gary?"

Gary: "No, we are the primary workforce in the organization."

Me: "Then why are you afraid?"

Gary: "I am not."

That day, Sagar was on a campus drive. Gary called him for advice on whether to send the reply email as I had suggested. Sagar advised against it, saying it would cause trouble. He said he would talk to me and asked Gary not to interfere. While Gary respected my leadership within the team on that occasion, he was hesitant to act. On behalf of Gary, I sent an email to the delivery team, emphasizing that a JD was essential for the recruitment process and asking for clarification on why doctors were needed in an IT firm. Manish was furious.

Sagar called and asked me to stop arguing over email, warning that the delivery team would go to any lengths to satisfy their egos rather than understand the logic behind my request. I sought a solution.

Me: "I sent eight Dermatologists, Sagar. They were all qualified. Why can't the delivery team explain the requirements to the doctors? How can they expect us to prepare them without the right information?"

Sagar: "It is their ego, Harsh. They want to maintain dominance."

Me: "I cannot work without a JD, Sagar. Nobody can."

Sagar: "Call the delivery team and talk to them directly. There is a big difference between communicating over a voice call and an email. Your emails come across as rude, even if you are being polite."

Me: "Fine, Sagar. I understand. I will call them."

Sagar: "Why did you even touch that requirement? Did I assign it to you?"

Me: "How long will we just let it sit on our sheet, Sagar? I wanted to tackle an unworked task."

The next day, Manish was in the office. We greeted each other.

Manish: "I do not get what your problem is, Harsh."

Me: "I believe in professionalism, Manish."

Manish: "Huh! As if we are all unprofessional."

Me: "I have my side of justifications, Manish. Once you are free, give me a call. We shall have a discussion in your cabin. I think you have got the wrong impression of me."

Manish: "Done! I would love to hear from you."

About 20 minutes later, I was called into Manish's cabin.

Manish: "Yes, Mister. Please explain your side."

Me: "See, during my experience at previous organizations, we had a very decent work culture. We communicated everything over email, regardless of its length. Here, it seems that detailed emails are taken as offensive. I do not understand why everything becomes personal when the discussion is about work. I was simply asking for a job description, which would make things easier for everyone involved."

Manish: "Work cultures vary from firm to firm. It is up to you to adjust to the environment. You cannot impose your ways on others. Regarding the JDs, we provided them to your manager, and you did not communicate with him."

Me: "I did. He forwarded a one-liner about the requirement."

Manish: "Yes, that is the JD. What more do you need?"

Me: "That is definitely not a JD."

Manish: "Look, you should have asked Gary for more details. We explained the positions to him orally."

Me: "That was six months ago. He said he does not remember it now."

Manish: "That is his problem. That is your inefficient team's problem."

Me: "It is a human problem, Manish."

Manish: "How absurd is it to think the doctors were coming here to treat real patients?"

Me: "I never thought that. Who said that to you? I guessed there might be an ergonomic reason for dermatologists to be coming in. I just needed clarity. I emailed you asking why doctors are needed in an IT firm."

Manish: "Let me clarify again. I told your manager earlier. Google has images of skin diseases. People browse using keywords related to their skin conditions. These dermatologists have to name the diseases based on the uploaded images to facilitate targeted browsing. It is a six-month contract job, 12 hours a week, with a monthly payment of x.x lakh rupees."

Me: "Wonderful! This is the information I was asking for. Now I can clearly explain to the candidates and send them in."

Manish: "Why didn't you call us to ask this? This fiasco could have been avoided."

Me: "As you said, I was carrying the work culture from the past. Thank you for explaining your work culture to me."

Manish: "You need to manage your aggression, Harsh."

Me: "I know, Manish. Since joining here, my life has been all about recruitment. Other HR teams went on trips, team lunches and drinks; we did not have anything like that, and I am getting frustrated with the routine."

Manish: "You need to plan your own trips and take frequent breaks. Do not let your personal troubles impact your work."

Me: "Thanks for the advice, and thank you for hearing my side. Have a great day."

Manish: "Take care and work on managing your aggression. You are really talented! Channel your talent in the right direction."

Me: "Sure! Thank you."

This conversation gaslighted me more than arriving at any amicable solution. Nevertheless, five dermatologists were selected from the eight candidates I sent, which was a significant achievement. Our competitors at FF, with their entire team managed six selections, while I alone secured five for CF. Gary appreciated my efforts.

Gary: "Woah! Congratulations, Harsh! You have done exceptionally well."

Me: "Thank you so much."

Gary: "What is with your interest in doctors?"

Me: "You know it better, Gary. I do not need to explain."

Both laugh

While I was successful in my part, the egos I had bruised in the delivery management were waiting for a chance to retaliate. I saw it coming. I got involved in another issue regarding the pay scale for pod-leads and team leads. We were asked to send all eligible candidates with team-handling experience. However, we were forced to convince team leads to accept the pay scale of pod leads once they were selected. This approach was counterproductive for the firm. When Sagar and I questioned this, the higher management told us to use common sense to understand the requirements. Such audacity is highly unprofessional and detrimental to any company. The arbitrary decisions negatively impacted our daily productivity. Sagar expected some action from the production side management regarding my conflict with the delivery side management.

It is not surprising that many Indians gain recognition only after leaving the country. Here, self-aggrandizement and self-interest often take precedence over the needs of the company or country. If one person knows more than another, jealousy often undermines company or national development. I do not wonder why Priyanka Chopra switched to Hollywood. As A.R. Rahman or Resul Pookutty noted, real politics in Bollywood starts after someone receives an Oscar or another major award.

In the book "The White Tiger," the concept of "The Rooster Coop Effect" is illustrated. This phenomenon explains why roosters get slaughtered one after the other—they do not have the mentality to rebel. This is similar to the majority of people in India. Roosters, or in this case, people, do not let others be innovative, effectively policing from within. This can be seen as "leg pulling" in layman's terms. This is also called as "crab in the basket" theory. It becomes very hard for an innovative individual to succeed. Many Indians fail in their innovations because we are caught hold in responding to the leg-pulling keeping aside the substantial work. This is why many Indians find success only after leaving the country. The West has minimal leg-pulling among peers. I believe it is true even with respect to many India based Nobel laureates who won their prizes only after leaving India. Am I wrong?

Today, dignitaries like Sundar Pichai and Satya Nadella are raising voices against state-induced atrocities in India, but they face disrespect and intimidation from ruling-party goons.[19] This indicates why India lags under the guise of being a "developing" country. Thoughts must open up before anything else. India skipped an important phase in its modern history. The West underwent 200 years of the Renaissance before industrialization. We adopted industrialization without achieving real intellect. In the West, someone who can afford a car knows not to honk in hospital and student zones. The Renaissance inculcated common sense most of all. In India, we adopted the growth model to show our success to the world, but did we educate the masses? Cosmopolitan cities like Delhi have the highest vehicular noise pollution, air pollution, land pollution and water pollution, yet its GDP is unbeatable by most Asian countries; but what is the use without life expectancy in the citizenry?

---

[19] NDTV, https://www.ndtv.com/india-news/citizenship-amendment-act-what-microsofts-satya-nadella-said-about-caa-2163499 14th January 2020.

Corporate firms in India often present a multinational facade, but internally, their culture can be quite parochial. They are resistant to meaningful reforms yet sensitive to trivial matters. For progress, minds must be open to change.

Initially, I enjoyed spending extra hours at the office because I had little else occupying my time. However, when I realized my efforts were being taken for granted and I was being exploited, I knew I could not stand for it any longer. I and Sagar unanimously and unequivocally declared that working on holidays was no longer acceptable.

With strong conviction, I sent an email to Gary, expressing my determination to reform the team and ensure its contributions to the organization were recognized. I asked him to forward this email to the AVP.

Hi Kris

Subject: A Recapitulation on the Deplorable Conditions of TAG

I hope this message finds you well. I am writing to address some crucial matters that have been overlooked by the higher management, which are impacting our recruitment efforts significantly.

1. Inadequate Job Descriptions for Key Positions

The recruitment team plays a pivotal role as the face of our organization and a revenue-generating unit. However, we are facing challenges due to the absence of detailed job descriptions for crucial positions. Understanding the requirements thoroughly is fundamental to our work, yet we often find ourselves lacking essential information. This results in miscommunication between candidates, interview panels, and the hiring team. For instance, I recently scheduled several dermatologists for interviews without understanding the specific demands of a software engineering firm. Such oversights not only waste our time but also reflect poorly on our professionalism. Hence, I urge the management to ensure that comprehensive job descriptions are provided for every new requirement promptly. Brief emails with minimal information are insufficient, as we require detailed insights to effectively engage with potential candidates.

2. *Apprehensions about CTC*

It is imperative that the compensation details for each position remain consistent and transparent throughout the recruitment process. Changing these details after candidate selection based solely on salary negotiations is unreasonable and undermines the integrity of our hiring process. We diligently share all relevant information, including expected salaries, with candidates during the interview stage. Therefore, it is essential that the offered compensation aligns with these expectations to avoid wasting resources on unnecessary interviews. I urge the management to establish and maintain clear compensation bands for each position to facilitate smoother negotiations and ensure that our efforts are not in vain.

3. Updates about revised positions not communicated

It has become increasingly difficult for us to effectively carry out our duties due to the absence of clear communication regarding the number and nature of vacant positions. We often find ourselves in the dark, only discovering changes to position requirements when they are updated on the open positions sheet without any prior notification. For example, this past week, we scheduled candidates for three female and five male Pod Lead positions, only to find out at the end of the week that the requirements had been revised to seven female and one male positions, leaving us with shortlisted male candidates for whom we had no suitable positions. This lack of communication not only disrupts our workflow but also undermines the integrity of our recruitment process. Furthermore, there have been instances of conflicting instructions and reprimands, such as being asked to schedule interviews for Assistant Manager positions at Apple Off-site, only to later receive criticism for doing so and being instructed to familiarize ourselves with the available positions. This inconsistency not only creates confusion but also constitutes harassment, which is unacceptable in any professional environment.

4. *Facilities for smooth functioning ignored*

It has become increasingly challenging for us to conduct interviews smoothly due to the unavailability of essential devices such as laptops and earphones. We are often forced to scramble and borrow these items from various sources, disrupting our workflow and causing unnecessary inconvenience. Moreover, this situation reflects poorly on our team and undermines the professionalism of our operations. The constant need to borrow devices not only disrupts our workflow but also exposes us to ridicule from both interview panels and project managers. We cannot continue to endure such embarrassment and frustration. We have raised this issue before, and it is imperative that a solution be found promptly. I urge you to either arrange for the necessary devices to be provided for interviews or acknowledge that conducting interviews without them is simply not feasible. Continuing to overlook this issue is not sustainable, and it compromises the integrity of our recruitment process.

5. *Working on holidays cannot be normalized*

I express my deep concern regarding the prevailing work schedule within the TAG Team, CF-BLR, particularly the expectation to work on weekends. It has become evident that working on Saturdays and sometimes Sundays has become the new norm for our team, with everyone being engaged in recruitment drives even during holidays. When I initially joined, I was informed that working on holidays would be occasional, to which I agreed, assuming that overtime pay would be provided. However, this has now become a regular occurrence, and it is unacceptable. I strongly oppose this practice of taking our human resources for granted in the pursuit of organizational goals. It is crucial to adhere to labor laws that stipulate the maximum working hours per week. Working on weekends deprives us of valuable personal time for hobbies, interests, social engagements, and personal commitments. This imbalance is unsustainable and detrimental to our well-being. While I understand that space constraints may necessitate occasional weekend work, it cannot be a permanent solution. We have previously proposed alternative solutions, such as providing other teams with a weekday off in exchange for working on Saturdays, to optimize space for recruitment drives. This approach offers several advantages, including:

a. *Improved utilization of space during peak recruitment periods.*
b. *Ensuring compliance with labor laws by balancing work hours across the week.*
c. *Enhancing employee morale and well-being by promoting a healthier work-life balance.*

I urge you to prioritize the well-being and work-life balance of the TAG Team members by revisiting our current work schedule and exploring sustainable solutions to address the space constraints without compromising our personal lives.

While I understand the demands of our roles, it is unfair to expect us to undertake additional tasks without adequate compensation. Every extra hour worked should be duly compensated monetarily. As an example, since joining, I have worked on 17 holidays, as evidenced by records from the holiday register and emails documenting interviews scheduled during Christmas and New Year's Day. While I have taken only 12 leaves, all of which fall under the compensatory category, I am still entitled to 5 compensatory leaves, in addition to my casual and other leave entitlements.

Another pressing issue regarding the location of recruitment drives and compensation for additional work within the TAG team.

Previously, the delivery team requested that recruitment drives be held in the parking area in front of the Bellandur office. This decision reflects a profound lack of understanding of recruitment processes and has serious implications that need to be considered:

*(i) **Reputation Damage**: Holding recruitment drives in such an inappropriate location risks tarnishing the company's reputation. Candidates may perceive this treatment as disrespectful, leading to negative word-of-mouth and potential damage to our employer brand.*

*(ii) **Security Concerns**: There is a risk of complaints being lodged against our team's manager for causing disruption in the VIP area, which could escalate into legal and security issues.*

*(iii) **Legal and Safety Risks**: Large gatherings in a public space without proper permissions pose a risk to public safety and may result in law-and-order issues, including breaches of security for VIPs.*

It is imperative that management reconsider this approach and collaborate with the TAG team to explore more suitable alternatives. Additionally, I would like to address the issue of compensation for extra work.

I urge management to recognize and compensate employees fairly for their additional efforts and to reconsider the location of recruitment drives to uphold our professionalism and reputation.

6.   TAG is devoid of non-monetary benefits also

The absence of recreational activities and team bonding opportunities. It has come to my attention that TAG does not currently offer any sports or cultural activities, nor do we organize team outings, lunches/dinners, or parties within the city. Additionally, off-site visits are not part of our routine. This lack of variety and social engagement in our work environment can lead to feelings of isolation and melancholy among team members. I urge you to consider the significance of this issue and take steps

Sagar cautioned me about the repercussions of my confrontations with both the production and delivery teams. My communication in emails was deemed highly offensive by the management, who seemed disconnected from ground realities. Despite the clear risk to productivity and the company's reputation, their egos overshadowed common sense. In response, the delivery team took charge of recruitment, challenging the TAG team to witness their resourcefulness.

While I advocated for necessary changes, Gary and Sagar acknowledged the impact of my activism but remained silent in their appreciation. They subtly advised me to refrain from involvement in fresher recruitment, as the delivery team took it upon themselves to prove their capabilities. Rishitha focused exclusively on fresher recruitment, while I handled experienced profiles for the week.

Daily walk-ins highlighted the challenges of recruitment without adequate resources. Delivery team never provided lunch to the waiting candidates, who were left to toil until the late evening without food. On one occasion, during the Holi festival, I was asked to oversee fresher interviews in Rishitha's absence. However, when I planned to leave early due to the holiday, a miscommunication led to accusations that I abandoned interviews midway. This issue escalated, with Sagar seeking an explanation. I defended myself with data, aligning with the delivery team's statistics.

I also raised concerns about the lack of hospitality towards candidates, highlighting the importance of transparency and humane treatment in recruitment processes. However, my outspokenness was met with resistance, as I was deemed 'ineligible' to voice such opinions as an Executive.

Despite the internal conflicts, external feedback from Srikanth and Lavanya recognized my potential beyond corporate walls. Their encouragement towards public service and politics was both humbling and inspiring.

XIV. Unprofessional Attacks

Gary came up to the Marathahalli branch just two days after the email argument. He asked to speak with me privately and led me into a room.

Me: "Yes, Gary. What is up?"

Gary (avoiding eye contact, speaking with low confidence and a quiet voice): "We decided not to make you a permanent employee from your current contract."

Me: "Okay. What did you decide then?"

Gary: "We decided to extend your contract for one more month."

Me: "Reason?"

Gary (clearing his throat to gather courage): "You are flirting with girls."

Me: "Excuse me, Gary! You know me well." (Gary stepped back a meter, sat down, and asked me to sit down)

Gary: "There are actually evidences that you are flirting during office hours."

Me: "I cannot accept allegations without proofs."

Gary: "I cannot provide them. By law, the name of the victim cannot be revealed."

Me: "Oh, you are talking law. Let me tell you, not revealing the name applies to sexual harassment complaints. But you are talking about "flirting" without any evidence. Is that a complaint?"

Gary: "Yes, it was a complaint."

Me: "Under sexual harassment? What is the ICC (Internal Complaints Committee) doing? Why am I talking to you?"

Gary: "No but I was instructed to warn you, and I did."

Me: "You are going against your own team member. Understand what they are making you do."

Gary: "You cannot talk to your manager this way, Harsh."

Me: "I want to meet the AVP on this matter immediately."

Gary: "The direction was from him."

Me: "I know. Hence, he is the right person to discuss this with, not you. I want to find out if this was a real complaint. If it was, this is not how the proceedings should take place legally. You are talking to an informed and responsible citizen. Moreover, you are a lawyer; get your facts straight and know the law before making allegations, Gary. Let me discuss this with the AVP and get back to you."

Gary: "You can. See, I never want to degrade you. You are like my brother, Harsh. I have always treated you as a younger brother and supported your growth. But today, I am ashamed to say my team has a flirt. We never faced such complaints before."

Me: "Leave it to me; I can clear this baseless allegation soon. Any complaints about my work?"

Gary: "Workwise, we have never had an issue with you so far."

Me: "Thankfully, you at least accept that."

Kris worked out a plan to expel me within another month. They wanted a replacement as efficient as me, making this extension necessary for them. The game was fantastic. Although I felt humiliated, I tried to fight. When they could not defeat me professionally, they attacked me personally, thinking I would succumb to such tactics and feel depressed. I messaged Kris that I wanted to talk to him in person, but he did not have the courage to face me and kept postponing the meeting for days. He played the game of unavailability, which is another toxic work culture besides micromanagement. While waiting for my appointment, I stopped working and told Gary I could take leave any day I wished without needing to provide reasons. He agreed since I had compensatory and casual leaves. Sagar remained silent, worried about his own job security throughout, although on the outset, he projected courage by keeping a draft of resignation on his mail. I openly started studying in the office, and Manish made faces at me while I did so.

Despite feeling humiliated, I planned a Saturday walk-in. Only three of us were to handle it: me, Harshitha, and Rishitha. Rishitha was childish, often talking innocently without reason. I treated her like a small kid; she was very cute and had just graduated a year ago. Harshitha was a determined and mature lady, smart and daring. During a break that day, all three of us went to the cafeteria. I was absolutely silent and serious.

Rishitha and Harshitha, pointing at me and planning to tease, asked, "What happened, handsome? Why so serious?"

Me: "Both of you tie a Rakhi (symbolic of a brother-sister relationship in India) to me."

Rishitha pushed her chair back and stood up. "What? Why would I tie a Rakhi to you, Harsh? Are you mad?"

Harshitha added, "What happened to you, Harsh?"

Me: "I got labeled a 'flirt' in the TAG team."

Rishitha: "Who dared to do that? You are so calm and talk to very few people. The real flirts are the delivery team leads and project leads who always bother me."

Me: "Did either of you complain about me?"

Harshitha: "You are disturbed, Harsh. Why would you think we would do something like that?"

Me: "Gary said some girl complained that I was flirting with her. I cannot figure out who it could be."

Harshitha: "Nonsense! Who would complain about such a workaholic guy? Despite all this, you organized a walk-in on our day off, today?"

Rishitha: "Sagar was so tense the other day because of your emails, Harsh. Gary called him a hundred times, not knowing how to handle your attitude. They could not do anything there, so now they are trying to lower your morale here, Harsh. Just ignore it."

Me: "I might resign once I find out who complained."

Harshitha: "No! The team needs you. You have brought so many changes. We need you."

Rishitha: "Yes, Harsh! We need you. We would not let you go."

Me: "I want to resign before they fire me."

Rishitha: "How do you know they are planning to fire you?"

Me: "They extended my contract for a month to find a replacement for me. How long are your contracts?"

Rishitha: "Four months, same as yours."

Harshitha: "I am on a permanent payroll."

Me: "Great. Let us go."

The following week, Bhavana and Harry came to my branch. Bhavana came to my bay to tell me she had received my contract extension letter and felt sad about it. It was the first time I saw her after she returned from her off-site trip.

Me: "Was it you who complained, Bhavana?"

Bhavana: "What are you even talking about, Harsh?"

Me: "You are the only one at work I have personal interactions with. There is a larger scope for a "complaint-category" involving you."

Bhavana: "Is this how much you trust me, Harsh?"

Me: "I do not know. Who could it be then?"

Bhavana: "I need to tell you something to show how much I support you behind your back. My ex-manager Mohini had a personal talk with me during her farewell, bringing up our proximity. The conversation went like this:

"Mohini: What is going on between you and Harsh? The whole office is talking about you two.

Bhavana: Positive or negative?

Mohini: Both. Why are you giving people a reason to talk?

Bhavana: People talk no matter what we do, Mohini. I think we should not care.

Mohini: Will you be able to handle the negative comments?

Bhavana: Harsh and I are both unmarried, and if we are together, it is nobody's business. We have never neglected our work, and neither of us has any work-related complaints. So, it is up to us, as we know what we are doing.

Mohini: That is nice, but be careful!""

Me: "Be careful? Really? What kind of people I am living among?"

Bhavana: "I gave her a firm reply."

Bhavana may be a good person, but I do not trust her at work, especially after the annual event. The conversation with Mohini she cited above was unbelievable and an utter shock because she was regularly going out with Manoj already. I was the first person who received their gossips all the way. She did not address that. Nobody is trustworthy here. So, I had my justification in not trusting her.

Me: "Bhavana, do not tell me all this. I do not trust anything anymore. You told Mohini that I am chasing you, and now you are saying this to appease me."

Bhavana (disappointed): "I do not know when you will trust me, or any girl for that matter."

Me: "Do not go there, Bhavana. Do not go near "any girl" thing."

Bhavana: "It was my fault for telling you this. I came here excited to see and talk to you, and you upset me."

Me: "You came to share your trip experience with everyone in this branch. Do not twist realities."

Bhavana left my bay and did not tell me when she left the office that day. I had to go to her hostel in the evening to soothe her. She refused to come downstairs, but I convinced her.

Bhavana: "Tell me!"

Me: "I sometimes behave this way. I cannot trust anyone easily."

Bhavana: "You will trust me if you forget your past. Be honest. What do you think of me?"

Me: "Be straightforward in your question."

Bhavana: "Do you think I go around with every guy like this? Do you think I do with others what I do with you?"

Me: "I do not mind if you do. Does my opinion matter to you? Also, I do believe, you do this with Manoj, Sagar and maybe others?"

Bhavana: "So, you came here to tell me this? I cannot believe it! I can never gain your trust in this lifetime, Harsh."

Me: "I am sorry if I hurt you but that is what I feel."

Bhavana: "Leave!"

Me: "Okay! Do not talk to me like we have declared exclusivity. Send me home with a smile, please. You look terrible when serious. I am already puzzled about who complained against me. I will get clarity once I speak to Kris. He has been avoiding me every day. Tomorrow is Tuesday; I will catch him."

Bhavana pulled me close, catching my collar, and closed her eyes. I kissed her lips briefly. She released me, and I looked around and up into the balconies to check if anyone saw us.

Bhavana: "I should be more worried. I live here. You do not need to look around."

Me: "I belong here; if any moral policing happens, you will go back to your hometown. I will have to handle it."

Bhavana: "Harsh! I cannot believe you said that. I am boldly doing this with you, and you think I would run away?"

Me: "That is how you girls are."

Bhavana: "Stop it, Harsh! Enough! Your ex may be a bitch, but not me. I am an Indian and proudly will remain. I have emotions, unlike her. I do not share myself with everyone like she did. You seriously need to move on from her."

Me: "Mind your words, Bhavana. I told you not to go there for obvious reasons."

Bhavana: "Come to me when you no longer need to remember her. Bye!"

Me: "Pshh! Wait! Come here! (I grabbed her into my arms) I am sorry; I do not want to send you inside with this mood. What do you want? Ice cream? Where shall we go?"

Bhavana: "Nowhere."

Me: "Then? Dildo?"

Bhavana: "Shhh! Quiet! I have clothes to wash today."

Me: "Fine! I will see you at the office tomorrow. I am coming to your branch anyway, to meet with Kris."

I texted Kris on Tuesday morning to check his availability at the Bellandur branch. He asked me to come by around 2 PM. I went there to meet him in his cabin. Our conversation went like this:

Me: "Gary mentioned something strange. What is the problem, Kris?"

Kris: "There are several issues, Harsh. Firstly, your long emails. Why waste time on them when you could work on the requirements? Secondly, I saw you flirting on the floor with a lady, and there was a complaint too."

Me: "Okay, if you think emails were wasting time, I must tell you that the inefficiency and poor management capacity in the organization is wasting time. Flirting? On the floor? Can you prove it?"

Kris: "Let us come to emails part, later. Yes, through WhatsApp chats on the floor."

Me: "Who is the lady?"

Kris: "I cannot reveal her name, but she joined about two years ago at the Marathahalli branch."

Me: "Does she sit inside the projects or outside?"

Kris: "Outside."

Me: "Got it."

Kris: "I knew you would figure it out. This is the issue. We concluded you were flirting based on chat screenshots."

Me: "Was this a complaint or gossip?"

Kris: "She showed it to her manager, who then brought it to me."

Me: "Why her manager and not me if there was a problem?"

Kris: "She did not have a problem. Her manager did. Girls boast. She is a senior analyst, and you are an HR. She boasted about HR chatting with her."

Me: "How is that an issue? You can see who pinged first in the chats."

Kris: "Yes, she did. But why respond during working hours?"

Me: "Our shift timings are different. My working hours are her non-working hours and vice-versa."

Kris: "For now, avoid chatting with girls even if they approach you."

Me: "That would be discourteous."

Kris: "That does not matter. Work is important."

Me: "I am in HR. My job is to interact with people."

Kris: "But not at the cost of the organization's reputation."

Me: "How?"

Kris: "First, tell me who clicks your pictures for Instagram."

Me: "Friends. Why?"

Kris: "I have heard rumors about you hanging out with a girl gang/group from the office after working hours."

Me: "That is not true. Those pictures are from various circles outside work."

Kris: "You have gangs/groups everywhere, so you might have one at the office too."

Me: "My life is an open book. I have nothing to hide."

Kris: "On-site contacts?"

Me: "Of course not. I have never visited on-site."

Without my knowledge I was justifying my private life outside, like I committed a crime.

Kris: "You should not have any chances. You are the face of the organization being in TAG. You should uphold its dignity. I do not want you to hang out with anyone from the office after hours."

Me: "For how long?"

Kris: "As long as you are here."

Me: "What if they approach me?"

Kris: "Tell them you will complain. Do not talk."

Me: "Should I have told everyone who complimented me at the office party that I would complain?"

Kris: "You should refrain from responding."

Me: "Fine." (It was useless to argue when he was being unreasonable.)

Kris: "Many women approach me, and I maintain restraint."

Me: "Oh!" (I meant that oh!)

Kris: "Another issue: you were caught by the police for drunken driving after the party."

Me: "The company did not provide transportation for the HR team."

Kris: "You should have left your vehicle and brought it the next day."

Me: "I had to drop Bhavana back to her hostel; she was my responsibility that night."

Kris: "By the way, did something ever happen between you and Bhavana?"

Me: "We are very good friends."

Kris: "That is it?"

Me: "Of course!" (I was offended by his insinuation)

Kris: "We have extended your contract by one month. Making you permanent depends on your behavior based on this discussion."

Me: "I cannot work on Saturdays and Sundays without pay."

Kris: "We will bring a reform on that from this financial year. Let me look into it."

Me: "Thank you."

I left the room in great disgust and met Harry and Bhavana outside in the balcony to share what happened.

Harry: "Who complained?"

Me: "Not a complaint at all."

Harry: "Then who is the girl involved?"

Me: "**Neelima** from Raghu's team."

Bhavana: I guessed it. You should have been more careful.

Me: "I was careful!"

Harry: "What did you do to her?"

Me: "Nothing. I never did anything to Bhavana yet, and what would I do to Neelima?"

Bhavana (shyly): "Harsh, how cute is that?"

Me: "I am erupting in frustration and you are getting romantic?"

Bhavana: "I am trying to cool you down with my romantic charm!"

Me: "Eff you!"

Bhavana: "You need not ask my permission to eff me, Harsh!"

Harry: "What else did Kris say? I heard you shouting inside."

Me: "A great humiliation. He has an attitude and education of homeless or sweepers. He is very cheap. Just like he brought his allies on huge pay scales into the organization, he was also surely brought here by some of his favorites earlier."

Bhavana: "Kris is an asshole. How did he become an AVP?"

Me: "I will plan a stand-up comedy routine about this. He should be ashamed."

Bhavana: "Great idea."

Me: "I am embarrassed to work here. He even asked if I had a girl gang from the office or outside."

Harry: "That is personal."

Bhavana: "Exactly!"

I later told Bhavana what Kris asked about us. These jobless clowns gossiped and spread rumors, indulging in micromanagement. They had nothing against my work, so they resorted to cheap tactics out of jealousy. Out of over an hour of conversation with Kris, we spoke less than four minutes about work. I met Gary downstairs to clarify.

Gary: "I did not know anything, Harsh. I followed directions."

Me: "The girl is Neelima from Raghu's team."

Gary: "Dangerous team. They've troubled others too. They were the reason Indira was fired."

Me: "I will talk to Neelima. Kris said it was a boast, not a complaint."

Gary: "I am really sorry, Harsh. I never wanted to degrade you. Good that you cleared things."

Me: "When the girl had no problem talking to me, why does it affect others?"

Gary: "Kris tried to make an issue of your 10-day leave. I covered it up because you worked on many holidays."

Me: "That is your duty to protect your team."

Gary: "Yes, I did."

I called Sagar to narrate my conversation with Kris.

Me: "I might resign. I cannot work under this AVP."

Sagar: "Have a drink, sleep well, and come to the office tomorrow. If you still feel the same, we will discuss your resignation. I trained you to stay, not quit."

I was made to feel guilty for being righteous. I was cornered, targeted, bullied, and harassed. The **trauma** made me delete all social life (which started just less than a year ago after the very long hiatus due to preparation) from Instagram, keeping only my lone pictures. THIS WAS TRAUMA RESPONSE. The next day, I spoke with Sagar.

Me: "All respect is lost. This was a well-played game."

Sagar: "You need work experience to fly abroad. Focus on that. Forget reforms and team well-being. Be selfish for six months and you will complete one year."

Me: "I cannot take this character assassination."

Sagar: "Chill! I faced all this and got fired in my earlier jobs. Yours is just a discussion."

Me: "I am blamed without reason. There is a difference!"

Sagar: "When someone cannot take you down professionally, they attack personally. This is why I asked you to be silent. You went to make reforms."

Me: "This is my personality. What is Gary doing after that cheap discussion?"

Sagar: "Boot-licking. I told him I trained you well, but he kept saying you were taking over his authority. He is worried you are skipping hierarchies."

Me: "What else can anyone do when a manager is incapable?"

Sagar: "Are you placing papers?"

Me: "Not yet. Let me either win or lose, but not quit."

Sagar: "Money is important to me. Experience is important to you. Take that and go. Let us not think about dignity."

Me: "I am not you, Sagar. My dignity and self-respect are more important."

Sagar's ego was deeply hurt by my statement, and we have been distant ever since. He became indifferent and, after discovering my caste through my Quora answers, he began to demean me based on it to lower my morale. Coming from a low socio-economic background, Sagar always felt insecure about his identity. When he learned that I belong from a caste which is both socially and economically forward, his insecurities manifested as derogatory comments about my background. Although I never believed in the caste system or religion, I found his behavior particularly offensive. Our relationship changed significantly—we no longer spent time together as we once did.

Quick Flashback

Raghu visited the Bellandur branch every Friday; he was interested in Bhavana. At first, he complimented her on how great she looked in black and asked her to wear black every Friday, which she did for months. However, he could not tolerate her getting close to me after I joined. His jealousy surfaced whenever we were together, and he tried to create trouble for me behind the scenes. To tease him, Bhavana and I would hold hands when he passed by and sit together in my bay. Unable to confront me professionally, Raghu attacked me personally. Adding to my professional reforms and revolutionary methods, Kris worked it out at a perfect timing. Here is what happened next:

Neelima, a girl from Raghu's project whose workstation was adjacent to mine, was an attention seeker and hyperactive, constantly passing comments about everyone. She targeted me one day, pretending to talk to her colleague but loud enough for me to hear her comment about my reading glasses, which I often wore on my forehead when not in use.

"Why does he put his glasses on his forehead?" she remarked.

I looked at her, but she quickly turned to her computer. I ignored it and went to Sagar's cabin to inform him about the unprofessional behavior.

"This is not roadside, Sagar. Why don't people maintain professionalism?" I asked.

"Did you feel offended?" he inquired.

"Not exactly," I replied.

"That's our rival group. They cause most of the troubles here, and our spineless manager does not stand up to them. What do you want to do now?"

"I want to know her details," I said.

"Come on, let's go to Kiran's Bay and find out," Sagar suggested. [**Kiran** is an associate in Admin team]

We discovered that Neelima had joined in November 2016, and other details such as educational background, experience, etc.

"Let's keep her under observation, Harsh. Let her slip up next time. Things are already heated. Let us wait for the right moment," Sagar advised.

"I feel helpless as an Executive. You are a Deputy Manager, Sagar. You can take action. How can I work confidently if you are afraid to protect your team?"

"Even if I speak up, our manager will shut me down, just as he does with you. We have no freedom here; it's a family business, and we have to follow the norms."

The next morning, Assistant Manager **Santosh**, accompanied by another female colleague from Raghu's team, rushed to my bay to inform me that a candidate I had placed a month earlier had absconded. Their tone was unmistakably judgmental, as though my competence was on trial and I was personally accountable for the employee's decision. I wanted to tell them that it is their toxicity that led to an employee's exit but I responded calmly, assuring them that I could arrange a replacement at the earliest.

Yet what lingered was a deep sense of revulsion at their entitlement—the expectation that human beings, like products, should come with warranties. The same afternoon in the cafeteria, Sagar was sitting with colleagues from various projects while I conducted interviews at my bay. Raghu entered and tried to flaunt his authority.

"Hey guys! Did you hear about the proposal to merge TAG under my control?" he announced.

"Why announce it here? Let us wait for the official notice," Sagar responded.

"You'll have to work under me," Raghu boasted.

"That day won't come. My resignation letter is ready to send," Sagar replied coolly, shutting Raghu up. Raghu left in embarrassment, and Sagar later narrated the event to me. We all laughed at Raghu's immaturity.

"A person who knows nothing about recruitment or management wants to take over TAG," I remarked.

"We should be ashamed, laughing at ourselves," Sagar said.

"Despite our sincere efforts and market reputation, every random person is attacking us," I added.

A few days later, Neelima made another comment, this time more directly, while I was in the cafeteria.

"Why so serious?" she said, looking into the air.

This time, I was not as offended. I checked her social media and found she was a talented dancer, with rhythm and expressions reminiscent of someone from my past. Although Neelima was different in many ways, her cheeks and eyes struck a familiar chord.

"I think I am impressed with Neelima," I told Sagar.

"Nice! She has gained your attention then," he said.

"Let me talk to her," I decided.

"You've fallen for her! Proceed. You have got a chance to move on from your past," Sagar encouraged.

"Don't generate feelings in me. I am happy this way," I said.

"They are already there. You just have to recognize them," Sagar replied.

"It's just attraction. I cannot love anyone right now," I insisted.

"Be careful. It is our rival group. Do not share any confidential information. Ask for theirs and keep me informed," Sagar warned.

"I know. Do not worry," I reassured him.

"I want you to have fun and move on from your past. She seems to like you," Sagar noted.

"This could be a honey trap. I should not rush," I cautioned.

"That's why I asked you to be careful. She may be a pawn in their game. Play safe," Sagar advised.

"I know right!" I agreed.

One evening, during a group meet at my bay, I saw Neelima passing by. I called her over and initiated a conversation, complimenting her dancing and demeanor. We started having regular casual talks and added each other on social media. We were invited to a birthday celebration in the cafeteria, where Sagar made me shy with his banter about Neelima.

Someone: Please come forward, HR team.

Sagar (with a mischievous smile): Harsh, step up!

That was loud and caught me off guard.

Sagar (softly near my ear): "Take a chance! Lead the way."

Me: "Sagar is the most charismatic person on our team. He should go first. Please, Sagar, take the lead!"

Sagar: "You have youthful charisma. My time has passed."

Raghu: "Come on, Harsh! Have some cake!"

Me: "Sure!" (I took a small piece of cake.)

Neelima: "That is all?"

Me: "Yeah, that is enough. I cannot have much cream; I am lactose intolerant." (I doubted she understood.)

Me: "Whose birthday, is it?"

Raghu and others: "Birthday boy and birthday girl, come here!"

Sagar and Me: "Happy Birthday to both of you!" (We smiled.)

During this celebration, Neelima and I exchanged phone numbers and switched our chat to WhatsApp. I even wrote a poem for her, admiring her beauty and dance expressions. This was the start of our closer interactions.

I See You

I see you, as a shower over the forest fire

I see you, as a raft in the deluge

I see you, as a riverine during my thirst

I keep seeing you no matter what

I see you, as a solace in my anguish

I see you, as a cheer amidst my wretchedness

I see you, to rehabilitate in you after a havoc

I keep seeing you no matter what

I see you, jealously when other guys interact with you

I see you, helplessly when you are reminiscent of my past-crisis

I see you, apologetically when you get offended seeing me watch you

I keep seeing you, no matter what

What I see, you may not see

What I see, might not be meaningless

Hence, I keep seeing you, no matter what

I showed her the poem the next day, and she thanked me for publishing it on my Quora blog. The line she loved most was, "jealously looking at her when other guys interact."

Neelima: "Is this really written for me, or are you just trying to impress every girl with the same poem?"

Me: "I can put your name in each line and republish it."

She held my fist tightly and looked into my eyes, saying, "No! I trust you!" The touch felt artificial though. The attraction seemed to fade without a spark in her touch. Despite this, she continued visiting my bay almost every day, engaging in casual conversations about pets and exchanging compliments. I updated Sagar on the situation.

Me: "I did not feel any spark in her touch, Sagar."

Sagar: "The story has gone that far? Touch? Wow, you are fast. Where did you guys meet?"

Me: "Nowhere yet. I asked her out, but she declined. So, everything has been at the office so far. She keeps coming to my bay."

Sagar: "Congratulations, bro! You will feel the spark when you are not surrounded by people."

Me: "Come on, I have no intentions. I am just attracted because she resembles someone from my past."

Sagar: "You need to see her as a different person. Do not project your past onto everyone, Harsh."

Me: "Are you encouraging me or getting me into trouble? I do not understand."

Sagar: "A happy person is more productive. I can imagine how sleepless your nights must be. You need to fill them with some happiness instead."

Me: "A happy person is more productive—hahaha! That is Elton Mayo's theory, in management studies. Let us see where this goes."

Sagar: "I do not know who Elton Mayo is, but I know Arjun Reddy. He kept crying for Preeti, but he did not miss an opportunity with other girls. Be like Arjun Reddy. Do not miss out."

Me: "Hahaha! Sagar, that is not my nature. I am vulnerable with everything going on in my personal life."

Sagar: "Chill! Enjoy yourself at work. Forget the rest. You know how I feel when I go home. That is why I avoid going home."

Me: "I know!"

So, this was the flashback. I never blame Sagar. I had my own brain, and his encouragement did not influence me much. My past had a greater impact. We are humans and attractions do happen. I was humanly attracted to Neelima because I am not a machine.

Into the Present

As always, Neelima walked to my desk. This time, she dropped a bombshell.

Neelima: "I am serving my notice period."

Me: "What?"

Neelima: "Yeah!"

Me: "Cool. What is next?"

Neelima: "I am planning to start a garment business. I want it to become a brand-level apparel store."

Me: "Congratulations! So, you resigned. I thought you were being fired too, like me."

Neelima: "What happened?"

Me: "I was told that I was "flirting" with you."

Neelima: "What? Who said that?"

Me: "I do not know if you are acting or if you really did not know."

Neelima: "Trust me, I did not know."

Me: "Alright. Your manager shared some of our chat with the AVP."

Neelima: "Yes, he asked me about it a few days ago."

Me: "Why did you share private details? You could have told me if you were uncomfortable."

Neelima: "Hey, I was never uncomfortable. He was just curious. I did not know it would escalate."

As Manish passed by, he gave me a look, indicating I was wasting time talking to the same girl again.

Me: "Come on, he saw us again."

Neelima: "This guy? Did he say you were flirting?"

Me: "No, he is different but from the same group."

Neelima: "Well, are we continuing to talk or are you taking this seriously?"

I looked at my computer screen and gestured for her to go back to her work. I deleted her from my social media and contact list. We never spoke again, even after she left the company. Sagar and I analyzed the situation and concluded that it did not start as a trap. It began with Neelima, but Raghu turned it into one, trying to pry into my personal life.

Management thought they could shut me up with character assassination, but I emerged unscathed. My reforms and attitude remained unchanged. Staying focused on goals is crucial despite hindrances. I was not the first victim of character assassination. Even great leaders like Nehru faced similar attacks. They called him a womanizer because conservatives could not fathom such a lifestyle; it went on to an extent that his cause of death was cited to be syphilis. My flirt-tag was similarly driven by jealousy. In developing countries, those who work diligently often face such challenges.

Why do these countries often become colonies? The answer lies in the lifestyles of their public, who habitually interfere in others' personal lives. Any authority that meddles excessively in personal matters will face negative repercussions. When a government spies on its citizens' food, dress, and worship habits, it hampers the economy. Similarly, a management focused on regulating employees' personal interactions will fail to understand the organizational environment. Such managements are bound to fail eventually.

XV. Pseudo Isolation

One midnight, I received a call from Bhavana, who insisted I write a poem about her. I told her I needed more time, but she was adamant.

Bhavana: "Is Neelima more important?"

Me: "I did not write it for Neelima. I saw someone else in her. I wrote it for that person."

Bhavana: "I do not care about all that! I want a poem about me."

Me: "Fine! You will find it in the book I write."

Bhavana: "Wow! Waiting."

I decided to pen down the story. I was not confident about standup comedy and unsure about the right platform, so I planned to write a book to expose whatever happened to me at this organization. The next day, Bhavana came to my branch, busy chatting with various project heads. In the conference hall, I found Harry dancing, and I joined in, singing songs.

Me (looking at Bhavana): "Bheegey Hont Tere! Pyaasa Dil Mera!"

Bhavana (hiding her lips): "Please sing the next lines without looking at my lips and body."

Assistant Manager (running away): "OMG! These HRs have gone wild!"

During the isolation period, I grew closer to Beulah, a friend from my dance group whom I treated like an elder sister. She was moving to the UAE soon. Whenever I needed to vent about office politics, we hung out. Meeting Bhavana outside the office became rare. I posted solo pictures with hashtags like "colleagues turned to friends" and "friends turned to partners" to irritate Raghu and Kris. The people with me were never in the pictures, and I did not add picture credits either. It was fun.

At work, I focused solely on my tasks. Even in my final month, I went to campus drives with Sagar and the team. Sagar rarely sat at my bay during this period. We talked less. He attended an interview with another company, anticipating action against him at CFs, but he was not successful as he applied in the delivery field. Sagar tried to ease the situation with me during a campus drive breakfast.

Sagar: "Harsh, do you know how famous you have become in all CF circles?"

Me: "Of course. I love stardom."

Sagar: "I do not know about your stardom, but there is a threat to the whole team because of your reforms."

Me: "I cannot pretend to be someone I am not, Sagar."

Sagar: "Ultimately, they will win because you are at the lowest position in the hierarchy, with exceptions to Rishitha and Harshitha."

Me: "I know. But who is afraid of whom now? The one who is right makes the news, is famous now. Am I making sense?"

There was dead silence. Everyone knew I was leaving after that month, but I was confident. Once I left that company, I knew I had various platforms to explore. I invested my time in knowledge and wisdom, which reaps long-term benefits. Those who cannot stand up for justice cannot expect others to stand up for them. We live in a society where supporting each other's rights is essential. Many great personalities have faced transfers, suspensions, dismissals, and even death for standing up for a cause. I am one such cog in nation-building. Corporates are not separate from reforms. During my tenure, I learned what not to do in apex positions; I learnt how not to run a business when I open up my own.

During another campus drive, a manager from Noida joined us to explain his project.

Noida Guy: "You are the one who was caught in the drunk driving incident, right?"

Me: "Yeah, that was proudly me."

All laughing

I realized how famous I had become. Everything about me was reported to the Indian Headquarters, but critical issues like job descriptions were ignored. A few days later, Gary **proposed** making my position permanent. He called me to discuss my pay, suggesting x.x LPA. I asked for x.x LPA. He said he would discuss it with Kris. I was no longer happy with the job, though. In that final month, I had an interesting recruit, **Amruta**, for the Soft-Skill Trainer position; she was a poet and writer. It was great knowing her. Pranay, also happened to be an avid reader, read about 50 books a year. He was also a poet. We shared our blogs and had intellectual fun.

During isolation, I felt as anxious as Kunal Kamra after his flight row with Cowswami.[20] I kept pushing reforms, despite the guilt from narrow-minded colleagues. They made me feel wrong for speaking up. Romeo troubled me with late arrivals and abrupt rejections. I asked him to provide detailed requirements and CTCs. He escalated, accusing me of directing him. I explained it

---

[20] BBC News, https://www.bbc.co.uk/news/world-asia-india-51291315 29th January 2020.

was common sense to provide job descriptions for recruitment. Gary warned me again during another walk-in drive about my emails.

Me: "I will keep doing it until I receive proper job descriptions, Gary."

Gary: "We have been working this way for over ten years. Why don't you understand?"

Me: "I do understand. You are talking about your generation's approach. I am talking about mine."

Gary: "You are directing managers on what to do and what not to do."

Me: "What kind of manager does not communicate his requirements? We do not know whether to keep working on the same requirements or if the vacancies are filled. He has not updated candidate feedback for months. How will we know if someone is selected or rejected? I discussed this with Sagar, and he suggested I escalate the issue. You can talk to him for further clarification."

Gary: "The mails should go through me, not you, for whatever reason."

Me: "You lack a spine, Gary. As an Executive, I am standing up for the whole team. Look at you, with your job insecurities despite having over a decade of experience."

Gary: "How dare you talk to your manager like this, Harsh?"

Me: "You cannot do anything more than fire me. I have already made up my mind. If you were a real manager, you would integrate employee goals with organizational goals. Despite so many issues, you never speak up. Today is Saturday, and here we are again after telling them countless times that I do not wish to work on holidays. Know where the fault lies. Stop yelling at your teammates. I have another batch waiting. Excuse me."

One of the projects planned an outstation official tour, and Harry also went. It was a two-day weekend trip. Other team managers were much more supportive of their team's recreational interests and mental health during weekends. Meanwhile, my team was hiring during and after the week, receiving reprimands but not recognition. Harry returned and planned a surprise party for Harshitha's upcoming birthday. Harry was close to both Rishitha and Harshitha as they spent most evenings together after work. I was connected to everyone formally, not informally. To our surprise, Harshitha herself invited us to her birthday party. Harry, who had great expectations from Harshitha, was taken aback when he learned she was living with another guy. He quickly shifted his focus to another lady that night, but even those expectations were dashed.

After my shift ended at 6:30 PM, I went to the Bellandur office. I did not take my vehicle as I knew I would drink. I became a pillion rider. Aparna, Harry, Rishitha, and I went shopping for a gift for Harshitha. Bhavana never joined parties involving Rishitha due to their rivalry. She even taunted me and Harry for being with Rishitha. That is another story. Bhavana, the sad and disappointed soul, went back to her hostel. We bought Fast Track shades for Harshitha. The party was at her house in KR Puram, and we were to arrive by 8 PM. After greetings and wishes, the first thing I demanded was music, which we arranged successfully. The drinks were ready, and dinner was to be bought: the delicious Kebabs from Residency Road, along with biryanis. We were about ten people in total, including Harshitha's old friends. Subhash and Venus were notable as they interacted a lot. One was Harry's friend Herbert, and another, Valli, was expected to join. They all knew each other from previous parties. I was the new one. Harry was eagerly waiting and practically drooling at the door for Valli. We all teased him for his awkward behavior.

Harry (sarcastically): "Shut up, all of you! What do you know about how much I am into her." (Sticks his tongue out like a jerk.)

Everyone was into Venus. She was the apple of everyone's eye, except Harry's. Venus had a different charisma. As time passed, the discussion turned sexual. I was in a "what the hell" mood when it started.

Me: "Okay, time to leave."

All: "Nooo! What? You have only had one beer."

Me: "That is enough."

Rishitha: "Sit down, Harsh. It is fun!"

Me: "What is fun? Writing a poem about one woman led to being tagged as a flirt. Who knows where this will go. I am out. I cannot deal with small minds."

Harshitha: "Exactly! They are immature fools with small minds, Harsh. They are targeting you for what you are not. Just drink and let it go."

Harry: "Fuck my manager!"

Me: "Why would I fuck your manager when my manager is already keeping me busy?"

(All laugh loudly.)

Aparna: "Gary should have been here."

Me: "At least here, Aparna! Please spare him."

Rishitha: "Okay, the bottle now. Your turn to question me, Venus."

Venus: "Who is your favorite hero?"

All: "What kind of boring question is that?"

Venus: "I skip."

Aparna: "No skipping. Let us restart the game."

Rishitha (to Venus): "Who did you have your first sex with?"

Venus: "My first boyfriend."

All: "So smart answer."

Subhash (to me): "When did you lose your virginity?"

Me: "27."

Venus (judgmental): "That is late."

Me: "Come on! I am demisexual."

Harshitha (to Rishitha): "Same question."

Rishitha: "I am a virgin and I do not want to be."

Aparna (to Harry): "What is your most memorable moment?"

Harry: "I am waiting for Valli. Do not ask me anything more." (We all kicked and punched him playfully.)

Harry (to Herbert): "Who do you like the most here?"

Herbert: "Rishitha."

All (hooting): "Brave you, Herbert!"

Rishitha: (humiliating way) "Yuck! Come on!"

Nobody should treat a man disgracefully when they complement and express interest in a woman. The next time will not be the same for that man; it crushes the confidence to make a move.

Me (to Venus): "What is your secret desire?"

Venus: "I do not have any."

Aparna: "That cannot be the answer."

Rishitha: "Yes, answer it!"

Venus: "I do not understand. Do you mean sexual desires or private desires?"

Me: "Anything. For example, I have a secret desire to date a transgender person at some point in my life. Something like that."

All: "Oooohh!"

Rishitha (high already): "Hero!" (Pulling my cheeks.)

Subhash (to me): "Who is your favorite porn star?"

All: "Hooooo!"

Me: "Mia Khalifa and Dani Daniels."

All: "OOOH! That is great!"

Venus (to me): "Have you ever had a one-sided love?"

Me: "NEVER" (I clearly lied)

Aparna: "Wow! Look at his confidence."

Rishitha: (hitting & pulling my cheeks)

Me: (irritated) "You are so high, Rishitha."

Aparna: "Now Harsh asks all the questions. We will answer."

Meanwhile, Valli arrived, and Harry became hyperactive. He energetically started participating. I kept everyone busy with questions for about an hour. At the end:

Me (to Rishitha): "Do you really think virginity is a concept?"

Rishitha: "Of course!"

Me: "Harshitha! Is that bedroom vacant? Let me explain it to you, Rishitha! Come with me."

Rishitha (slaps my back and hits my head): "Come on, Harsh!"

Me (to someone, not revealing the name): "Any untold story to share that you have never shared before?"

Someone: "I once had extramarital sex when my husband was out of town."

All: "Wow! That is okay! We will forget it here. We never heard you say it."

Me (to Aparna): "What do you like most about me?"

Aparna: "Your husky voice."

Me (to Valli): "Do you prefer sex with someone experienced or inexperienced?"

Valli: "Of course, experienced."

Harry: "What is wrong with inexperienced? We are hornier."

Valli: "Feeling horny and making someone horny are different. Explain that to me, and I will accept you are better than the experienced."

Harry: "I will tell you once you allow me."

Me: "Harry, you are drunk. Lol."

Harry: "No! She is underestimating me."

Valli: "Okay, show me what you got."

Harry: "Here? I am from a traditional family. Not here."

All: LOUD LAUGHTER.

Valli: "Harsh, how experienced are you?"

Me: "Depth cannot be measured in numbers or time."

All: "OOOOOOOO! Harsh!"

Aparna: "Had heartbreak? Looks like he has not moved on."

I told them how it ended overnight. Rishitha and Valli were the most moved because they could relate. Rishitha cuddled me to console me, even though I was not crying. She seemed to be knowing that pain. The atmosphere turned very serious. Valli picked up her heartbreak story and that was the longest of all our conversations for the night. We were all high and craving food. We all plunged into dinner. Afterward, we went downstairs for smokes. Throughout dinner and after, Harry was trying to hit on Valli.

Me: "Something is missing."

Harry: "Rishitha."

Me: "Oh yeah!"

Without realizing, Rishitha and I had been cuddling since my story. She kept asking if I was okay every single minute. Even while standing, we cuddled. Harshitha's cake had lactose, and I got slight cramps. Despite being drunk, Rishitha showed great care. She stood at the washroom door until I came out and called me after she went home to check on me; she left early as she had to drop Venus off. Meanwhile, Harry was in cuddles with Valli already. They looked sweet together.

Our conversation downstairs turned to office politics and how I was cornered.

Me: "Gary ki maa ka L."

Valli: "Whose mom would have an L? Why do you use such meaningless profanity?"

Harry: "My manager's maa ka L."

Valli: "Ehh! I just asked to rectify, right? Uski maa ki C."

Harry: "Okay! My manager's maa ki C."

Subhash and Aparna threatened Harry, saying his verbal abuse was recorded and would be sent to his manager the next morning. He took it seriously for a few minutes until they revealed they were just joking.

Harry: "So what? Am I supposed to be scared? Give it to me, I will show it to him myself."

Harry was such a funny and sweet guy. He really made the night. We decided to leave, and as we went to pick up our belongings upstairs, an interesting conversation unfolded.

Valli (picking up her bag, standing at the door): "Harsh! Are you interested in a one-night stand with me?"

Me (at the distant end, near the dining table, clearing the plates): looking blankly at Aparna, Harshitha, and Harry

Harry: "I am coming too. We will have a threesome."

Aparna: "Harry is such a spoiled brat."

Harry: "Am I spoiled just for wanting a threesome? Look at Valli, suggesting one-night stands!"

Me (still astonished): "Please do not mind, Valli, I am demisexual."

Valli: "That is okay! At least come and see my house. I am inviting you. Harry is invited too."

Me: "Sure."

Harry: "Let us go dude, Harsh. Valli's cuddle was so warm. Tonight is threesome. I made up my mind."

Valli and Harry knew each other way before and they evidently liked each other too. I was still in shock why Valli asked me for a one-night stand in front of Harry. On the way back, Valli kept flirting with me and Harry while Aparna and Harry kept countering her. It was a wonderful night.

After everyone left, Harry, Herbert, and I went to Valli's house. We had a long conversation before she went into her bedroom to take a call from her brother.

Me: "Harry, let us leave, please. I am afraid."

Harry: "Let her initiate something, dude."

Herbert: "What about me?"

Harry: "You can leave, Herbert. It is a threesome tonight."

Me: "Fuck you, Harry!"

Harry: "Imagine Neelima and proceed, dude!"

Me: "I never had anything to Neelima. I cannot just touch some random person. Besides being demi, I am a hypochondriac too. Valli could have anything like HSV, HPV and so on. STIs are serious and can haunt you for life. Listen to me, it is good for you too."

Harry: "Is it? She does not look like she has anything."

Me: "I suspect she has herpes dude. Observe her lips when she comes out now. I could discuss it with her openly but I am afraid she turns defensive at this point when she is drunk. Nobody looks diseased. It is in their bloodstream. I would not let you do anything with her."

Harry was convinced. As we reached the entrance and were putting on our shoes, Valli came out of the bedroom in a hot nighty. Harry's jaw dropped, Herbert tried to cover his eyes, and I was laughing.

Valli: "What is happening?"

Harry: "Harsh is feeling very drowsy."

Valli: "He can sleep here tonight."

Me: "I need my medication. I accidentally swallowed lactose, looks like. I have to go home for that. I will call you tomorrow. Let us plan another party this weekend."

Valli: "Sure! Take care! Harry should come too. We will plan. Good night."

That was a legit escape. Harry and Herbert dropped me home safely. I thanked Harshitha for organizing such a great party before going to bed. The next day at the Bellandur branch, we found out Harshitha took leave, claiming she had contracted chickenpox. We were all discussing it in the cafeteria.

Aparna: "Harshitha was fine until midnight. How did this happen so suddenly?"

Rishitha: "She said her father came to pick her up; she must have left town."

Aparna: "Valli and Subhash asked if I was interested in recruiting people through the backdoor. They said they would bring candidates and give me 50% of what the candidates paid."

Rishitha: "Yeah, they asked me too. Did they talk to you about that, Harsh?"

Me: "No!"

Aparna: "Their interest in Harsh was different."

Me: "Come on, I made a great escape."

Rishitha: "What escape?"

Aparna: "Ask him."

Me: "Do not ask me."

Rishitha: (annoyed) "What is it? Will someone tell me?"

Aparna: "Valli asked him for a one-night stand."

Rishitha: "Really, Harsh?"

Me: "But I do not understand why Rishitha and I were cuddling so much."

Rishitha: "Do not remind me of that. Even I do not know. Leave it, just forget it."

Aparna: "Harshitha and Subhash are living together. Subhash is married with kids, but they are doing it so boldly!"

Me: "Let us not get into their private matters. As long as Harshitha knows about him completely and it's consensual, it's none of our business."

Rishitha: "High five, Harsh! I agree with you."

And reality was soon to unfold before our eyes. By the way, I went to Bellandur that day to talk to Gary about something serious.

Me: "Gary, we discussed the pay earlier, but there is a family emergency. I need about a month's break before I start on the permanent payroll."

Gary: "Harsh, a month is too long. And I discussed your request for a pay increase with Kris. He is not sure yet. Anything can happen."

Me: "That is okay, we still have time. I do not want to start work ASAP. You all demoralized me to the point that I have lost interest in this office."

Gary: "Come on, do not get demoralized, Harsh. I will try, but I am not sure. Kris will decide."

Me: "Alright."

The leave was not really for a family emergency, but for my alternative career, where I had no one above me to dictate my decisions. My plans were always big and long-term. For someone who invests many years in education, the world seems small and full of opportunities. I knew nobody would provide a one month's leave. My intention was to leave the organization eventually in the pursuit of something meaningful. I chose a powerful field where I could voice my thoughts. I entered the legal career. The examinations that I was preparing and studying for, at the office, were for law. I decided firmly that this life is for public service and fighting for justice. This experience at CF opened my eyes even widely to what my purpose in life was.

XVI. Twisting Surprises

A new project ramped up with a huge requirement: 150 freshers, 5 team leads, 10 pod leads, 1 manager, and 2 assistant managers, among others. We had over 120 candidates in the pipeline ready to be onboarded, with 30 more plus buffer candidates to be recruited. However, as we opened the sheet to call candidates and check their availability, we found that the names were overwritten and mismatched across different sheets. We could not understand why this happened or where things went wrong. Initially, we thought it might be due to duplication of efforts by team members, but that was not the case. The reason was beyond anyone's imagination: the data sheets had been manipulated, and the names were replaced.

An investigative committee was set up. All of our accounts, emails, and login details were scrutinized. It was found that Rishitha and Harshitha had edited the sheets. They were called in for interrogation. Rishitha was declared innocent because it was proven that Harshitha had Rishitha's login information, as Rishitha never logged out after her sessions from her PC.

Harshitha initially did not come to the office, claiming she was out of the city. The team threatened to send the police to her house, prompting her to come in immediately. It turned out she neither had chickenpox nor was she out of the city. After an 8-hour grilling session, she continued to resist the pressure. Ultimately, she was let go because the company's reputation would be at stake if the matter hit the market.

Meanwhile, candidates started walking in to check the status of their placement. These were candidates from Harshitha's end whose names were on the manipulated sheet. They threatened Gary, saying injustice could not be tolerated as the TAG and CF had assured them jobs through backdoor channels and collected money. The list included about 45 candidates from whom less than a lakh each was collected, depending on individual capacity. However, only 10 had the courage to confront the firm about their jobs. The team sent them away, telling them to catch those who assured them of jobs. The total amount in the scam earned by Harshitha & Co. was about 35 lakhs. The CF's management was shocked. These were youths who had sold their bikes, gold chains, borrowed money, or used hard-earned savings from parents and partners, only to fall into the hands of a job racket. Yes, we had been friends with a job racket all this time.

How did the scam surface?

1. Aparna informed Gary about Harshitha & Co's offer.
2. Digitized data of all the candidates walking into the company helped easily identify
3. Selected candidates' Aadhar numbers were collected once their selection was confirmed from our end that enabled tracking easy

Thus, the data could be compared with the manipulated sheets, and the scam was caught. But who was ultimately at fault?

1. The lethargic, feudal AVP who made selections based on narrow caste and regional inclinations. Had he hired Cathie as per my recommendations, the firm could have had an efficient recruitment team. He felt she was "too forward."

2. Corruption: No background verification had been conducted for supportive/HR/non-billable staff. But nobody knew where that allotted budget went. The 2-year experience Harshitha claimed was fake, which served as a slap in the face of Kris.

History shows that egoistic authorities are bound to self-destruct due to their insular nature against innovation and ideas. Internal corruption can outweigh every progressive objective. This felony was kept from leaking outside the team to protect the AVP's position, but my misdemeanor of drunk driving reached the Noida staff. These are the odds of totalitarianism.

Guess what?

The job descriptions started hitting our inboxes from all the managers whenever new requirements arose. This was a huge success after all my struggles. As long as the TAG team exists in Bangalore CF, my contribution will be remembered. <u>I taught both</u>

the vassals and overlords the professionalism of democracy.
Despite this, not even Sagar congratulated me. Recognition was
entirely absent, both within the team and for the team.

My Reward

Rishitha, Harry, Aparna, and Bhavana were counseled to avoid
my influence. I was referred to as a "case", along with Harshitha.
We were used as illustrations of what not to be. Bhavana informed
me about these developments and also gave me a heads-up that
my contract would not be extended and my employment would
not be made permanent. I was mentally prepared for it and was
not surprised. The real surprise was for those around me,
wondering how an efficient employee was being let go. When the
official notice came, Gary and **Phani**, the new Core HR manager
(Kris's lackey), called me into the room and informed me about
my non-continuation. I asked for reasons, and they had none. They
were guilty of their cowardice. I enjoyed cross-questioning them,
and they ran out of the room without answering any of my direct
questions. I pinged Kris again to talk, but he kept postponing.

Another Twist

Bhavana informed me that a new contract-based employee was
joining the TAG team the following month. I asked who it was,
and it turned out to be Ms. Indira. Gary brought her back as she
had not found employment elsewhere due to her lack of skills.

Gary's recommendation was her only option. She was delighted I was leaving, and I was pleased she could not thrive outside her patron's protection.

Last Days

My last working day was April 30th. I started taking pictures with everyone from all the projects two days prior. I was on good terms with everyone, and my departure-to-be shocked many. Nobody believed I was leaving, thinking I was joking because it was the end of April. Bhavana visited during my last few days. I informed every passerby about my last day, but nobody believed me.

Bhavana: "See! Nobody believes that you are leaving. We all know what you are, how your work was, and what your contribution to this firm is. Just because you hurt 1-2 people's egos, you have to go. You should have thought twice before sending those emails."

Me: "I do not do anything without thinking. I am taught to take a stand for justice. Here, I stood for the team. Now we started getting the JDs."

Bhavana: "Did the team stand for you?"

Me: "Not necessarily. But they are enjoying the benefits I made possible. Gandhiji, as a leader was used by the masses for their purpose to be served, and once done, they assassinated him."

Bhavana: "Gandhiji was glorified. You are demeaned. They have destroyed your career and your dream of moving to the West. Think about that."

Me: "Gandhiji is glorified only in the intellectual circles. Conservatives humiliate him. However, I have better options waiting for me. You know my venture into law. I have wonderful opportunities out there. Wherever illogical authoritarianism exists, careers are bound to be destroyed. Like in Bollywood, where an old flop actor hinders young talented Arijit Singh's career. Such conceited autocrats fail to realize their time will end sooner or later, and people will retaliate."

Bhavana: "You do not understand what I am trying to say, Harsh. People do not know why you are leaving today. They do not even believe it. But once you disappear, they will start talking about you and speculate about your sudden departure. They would not remember your hard work or your emails. They will only focus on the character assassination episode."

Me: "Let them! It is a game. This time I lost, next time, I will win."

Bhavana: "This is the saddest day of my life. You do not know how I feel."

Me: "Look, this is not my world. I have much more to deal with outside than you all do here. I do not care at all. Why are you so worried? I am relaxed."

Bhavana: "You acted hastily. You should not have skipped hierarchies and created a ruckus. You should have dealt with it like earlier how you got Indira fired."

Me: "That was different. I acted from behind because I thought I needed this job to grow. Later, I realized I was among a flock of sheep."

"Live like a lion even if you live for a day. There is no use living like a sheep for a hundred years." - Tippu Sultan

Bhavana: "Lol. Those sound too good in books."

Me: "I know I am bookish. But I do not worry much. I somehow feel you are also involved in all this behind my back."

Bhavana: "What?! Your suspicion started again?"

Me: "Of course. Nobody else is so bothered, and you are acting too concerned. It shows your guilt."

Bhavana: "That is because nobody knows you are leaving. They feel that you are joking. Who else will feel your absence?"

Me: "Many people. There are many who admire me. I do not want any drama from you. Keep it simple. I know you would not care the minute I am out of here."

Bhavana: "You know what? I failed drastically in one aspect."

Me: "I know. Gaining my trust."

Bhavana: "Remember me as a part of your life once."

Me: "Such a drama queen you are!"

That same evening, I happened to catch Kris when he visited the Marathahalli branch. I told him I wanted to take a photo with the great hardworking personality of the firm. I did not want to discuss the reasons for my departure anymore because I was ready to leave. I kept it casual. He began by discussing Harshitha's debacle, criticizing his own judgment for not seeing through her during the interview. I added salt to the wound by mentioning that her experience certificate was fake. This led him to recount his betrayals in life, where people often fled with his money. He seemed emotional, but I kept smiling. He acknowledged my 175% performance improvement during the contract extension period.

Me: "Good that you noticed. Thank you."

Kris: "Of course, you did exceptional work for us, but there were small things we could not get along with. Those were not issues but... just give me some time. I will want to see you back on board."

Me: "Oh! I have one last vacancy to fill in the admin department before I go. I will just do that and complete my exit formalities tomorrow. I never leave anything undone."

Kris: "Great! We admire this attitude, but you implemented it elsewhere too, where the troubles actually started."

Me: "Well, thank you. It was a pleasure working with you all here."

Grand Farewell

The farewell was unprecedented. Everyone wanted to see if it was true that I was leaving. Staff from both branches attended, including Indira and Manish. They all showered praises for my work, and testimonials were given. Amrita praised me for working seriously even on the last day. Srikanth expressed his sorrow, saying he would miss me and my contributions. He added that I acted like a right hand to their project. I delivered a speech, thanking everyone for giving me exposure to the "real corporate" world in India. After the cake-cutting ceremony, I danced one last time with my dance group to the same songs from the annual event. It was a great farewell. The last day was most memorable.

I went to the Bellandur branch to finish my exit formalities. I left with my dignity and self-respect intact. I uploaded all the pictures with everyone on Facebook, on purpose. Another twist arose. Harshitha and her associates found out that my contract was not extended and tried to connect with me. They arranged a personal meeting with Gary under the pretext of proving Harshitha's innocence. The same group informed me that "our time has come to avenge against Gary." Without delay, I called Gary and warned him to avoid meeting with Harshitha's team. I saved Gary from being beaten up that evening. I had no obligation to rescue him, but my principles came into play again. I left on good terms with everyone, even those who had harmed me. They deserved to see me succeed, so I kept in contact. I faced post-traumatic stress disorder (PTSD) for more than 18 months in relation to my character assassination at CF. It took me a great courage to come out of it. The therapists were judgmental, and the dilatory legal mechanism deterred me from accessing justice. There is a great suffering in such barbaric country. I somehow always still think of giving back my part to India, which although took away everything from me.

Nevertheless, the more I was oppressed and targeted for destruction, the more I achieved. Many people remained stagnant; their complaints never-ending. Their dreams of starting their own businesses were never realized because they never took that crucial step towards risk.

"He who is not courageous enough to take risks will accomplish nothing inlife." – Mohammad Ali

Like many, I shared my dreams in casual conversations at CF. I vividly remember two team leaders from Manish's team, along with Sagar, trying to discourage me.

"See Harsh, take it from us and remember our advice as you go; not everything in life goes as per our plans. We also had big dreams, but life had its own plans. We are nearing our 40s and look where we are. This is the hard reality. Better not carry so many expectations."

I responded that I make my plans work, while all three of them exchanged knowing smiles, reflecting their defeat in life. I moved on. Rishitha faced the same fate as I did, with Indira and Bhavana behind her termination. Rishitha called me in June to vent her anger against them. Around the same time, a senior executive from the Core HR Team texted me about my availability. I suspected it was Kris searching for a replacement for Rishitha. I told her about my busy schedule with my new career. Although my civil services dream did not realize, my public service aspirations lasted.

In the Aftermath

I was deeply absorbed in my legal career, spending more time at the High Court than in the classroom. In my second year of legal studies, I filed a public interest petition against the ruling government in the State's High Court over an environmental matter. I became involved with various national NGOs working towards building the Green Party in India, and my activism started to challenge the governments this time, let alone the corporates.

Balancing my legal pursuits with resolving family issues was overwhelming. I had primary responsibility for my younger sibling's career, which was also disrupted by my toxic immediate and extended family. Nevertheless, I settled my sibling down in the US with great effort. The COVID-19 pandemic further derailed my progress, pushing my goals years behind. The strain led to severe, long-term depression, compounded by setbacks in both my personal and professional life. During the lockdown, dealing with narcissistic family members triggered severe self-harming tendencies, and I fell back into greater degree of autistic spectrum disorder (ASD), reminiscent of my adolescence. My career in the aviation industry had been destroyed back then, and now my prospects in civil services faced a similar fate; both the times due to the family responsibilities that were above & beyond my age & capacity came up on my shoulders. I was dealing with high functioning depression since 2016 already; now that turned into heavy clinical depression.

Three years after leaving CF, I moved to England, carrying a heavy burden of social inferiority, low self-esteem, self-harming tendencies, heavy anxiety disorders, ADHD, ASD, C-PTSD,

ORD, and OCD. It took a long time to muster the courage to engage with others on daily basis; the abuse and discrimination in the Indian society had left me deeply scarred. I lived in vulnerability for years after escaping India, losing the confidence I had built in my twenties through education. Battling depression, I felt inadequate in public debates and discussions. I always felt like I lost purpose in life; this feeling was severe because this was the second time my goal was displaced. Finding a new career each time as we grow old is not easy. The academic interests and quest for knowledge I once had were gone, replaced by overthinking, burnout, and therapy. I considered waking up alive each morning as an achievement.

Despite these challenges, I made progress, albeit slowly. I always competed with myself from yesterday to have a better version today. I entered a Russell Group institution, earned merits and distinctions, and attended the 30th United Nations Human Rights Advisory Committee meeting in Geneva as a student delegate. I made valuable contacts at the Supreme Court of India. I assist in writ jurisdiction staying abroad and began receiving invitations for guest lectures at eminent institutions in India. I became a director in a social entrepreneurship firm in India. If at all I go back to India in the near or distant future, I have clear objectives laid down. The wheels were moving in the right direction, yet the imposter syndrome held me back.

I have worked in diverse workplaces in England and generally find white cultures to be mature and welcoming. Of course, there are exceptions with a few bad apples, and con artists and toxic individuals that can be found here as well. I come across boot-lickers and clowns, who are immature and inefficient often. I will try to release another work later in detail about the work cultures in England. However, the issues in these workplaces are different and not as petty as those often encountered in India. The problems here are more of mere personal than organizational. Most problems can be resolved within one conversation in the management higher ups due to the advanced understanding levels of people here and most importantly because of strong trade union presence as well as the systematic enforcement of employment laws. Work is not largely affected by egos, emotions, or personal grudges unlike in India where emotions determine everything in politics, society, work places, educational institutions, and so on. My rationale, logic, and hard work are highly respected in the West. Nobody bothers if I have a girl group or a boy group to hang out with. Nobody has time to really stalk my Instagram or Facebook to check who I am going out with or dating. Even if I go forward to share my interest in someone, I am always appreciated and encouraged. Mental health is taken care of highly. The West taught me to wear my failures as badges of honor. I feel safe here, where human life and values are respected. My intellect, ideas, and vision are recognized and appreciated, even though I have utilized less than 3% of my potential compared to my civil services preparation. My current focus is on personal growth and improvement. I aim to regain my concentration and consistency. It is strange to realize that the country I dedicated my entire life to, ransacked me and cast me out with nothing, while it is a foreign land that is now helping to rebuild me. Experience, especially life experience, never goes to waste. To all those who put me down, I would want to tell them through this work that I am successful with my progress. Success is the best revenge, and it never comes to ordinary people.

9 798894 467009